Digital Hypnotherapy

Feb 22

Andrew Archibald
www.hypnosis.scot

DIGITAL HYPNOTHERAPY
THE VIRTUAL PHONE APP METAPHOR

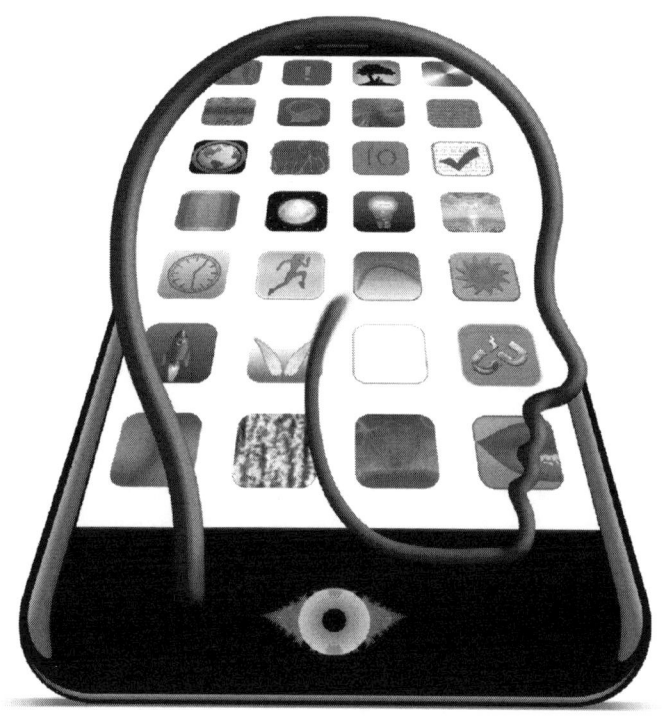

**Easily Create Effective Hypnotherapy Scripts
Extremely Adaptable Modular Framework**

Andrew Archibald

SINGLE EYE HYPNOSIS

Digital Hypnotherapy
The Virtual Phone App Metaphor

Andrew Archibald

ISBN: 9781914090110

Copyright © 21st Century Andrew Archibald
Single Eye Hypnosis
www.hypnosis.scot
singleeyehypnosis.com

Published by The Magic Road
An imprint of Leamington Books
32 Leamington Terrace
Edinburgh
EH10 4JL

All Rights Reserved. No part of this publication may be reproduced, stored in a retrieval system or transmitted in any form or by any means - electronic, mechanical, photocopy, recording or any other - without the prior written permission of the publisher.

Cover and interior graphics by Single Eye Hypnosis
Printed Edition

Contents

Legal Disclaimer	7
Digital Hypnotherapy	9
Why does Hypnosis Work?	13
The Self-conscious Mind and The Unselfconscious Mind	21
Addressing the Unselfconscious Mind	25
The Use of Scripts in Hypnotherapy	28
Digital Hypnotherapy Script Structure	30
Easy for You to Say	32
Inductions	35
You Are Breathing	36
Your Own Face	40
Deepeners	43
A Bell Rings Behind You	43
Triple Dream Sequence	51
Log cabin home	51
On the train	52
At the beach	53
Blackboard Portal	54
A: Avenue of trees with path	57
B: Beach scene	59
'Updating Apps' Modules	61
Setting the scene	62
Finding the device	62

Explaining the nature of the device	63
Finding the relevant or appropriate 'app'	63
Opening the 'app'	64
Updating the App Settings	65
Review After Updating	65
Backing up the Updated App Settings	66
Addressing the Subconscious	66
Exduction	67
Full 'Updating Apps' Scripts	69
Neuropathic Pain	73
Fear of Flying	89
Stopping Smoking	103
Bladder Control	123
Stamina (Running)	137
Increasing Self Confidence	151
Weight Loss	169

Legal Disclaimer

The contents of this volume do not provide or claim to provide medical advice, and nothing herein is intended to be a substitute for medical advice, diagnosis or treatment. First seek the advice of a medical professional or your own doctor and consult with him or her before making any changes to advised treatment.

Hypnotherapy products (videos, recordings or scripts) are not recommended for those experiencing mental disorders or illness. Those with a history of epilepsy are disencouraged to use, view or listen to any of the scripts available in this volume without first consulting and getting approval from a medical professional.

Never use the content of this volume (contents, scripts, etc.) or the content of those websites to which it may be linked whilst driving or operating machinery or equipment.

No guarantee as to the efficacy of the products or services in this volume, or the products or services in any website linked to through this volume, is either given or implied.

Digital Hypnotherapy

Presented in this small volume is a niche approach to hypnotherapy along with several detailed, working examples, aimed primarily at the younger generation, but also appropriate for anyone familiar with a smart-phone or tablet.

This method comprises a sequence of visualisations the model for which most young people are already intimately familiar. It's something that the young intuitively understand and with which they feel completely comfortable and at home.

In working with hypnotherapy clients, it quickly becomes clear that, generally, the older the client, the better read they are and therefore the richer their vocabulary. From this wealth of knowledge of the lives of characters drawn from literature (great or otherwise) and biographies those who have read broadly can draw much second-hand experience to add to their own first-hand experience.

Through no fault of their own, younger people are less familiar with literature of any type than their forebears since the reading of such works seem no longer to be regarded as integral to the educational curriculum.

The telling of stories to children by their parents or guardians would also appear to be an increasingly rare event. An ever-diminishing amount of time is given over to this in our modern life. Other, more excitingly attractive and automatic child-minding devices such as televisions, tablets and smart-phones are rapidly gaining preference. In this way younger people, in contrast to those of previous generations, are more likely to miss out on the type of inter-generational interaction and learning that traditional story-telling, vital to an interest in reading, than their elders enjoyed and from which they greatly benefitted.

In this way younger people are either less conversant with (or in some cases completely unaware of) the significant words, phrases, ideas, symbology and allusions which are inherently meaningful to those who are either older or those who have read more broadly.

The approach presented in this short volume was born from a need to create a metaphorical framework which younger clients in particular, whatever the depth of their knowledge of literature, traditional fairy tales or myth, would find easy to visualise, understand and accept.

Smart-phones have become ubiquitous and, with the increasing saturation of the market with ever more sophisticated devices capable of an ever-rising number of functions, the vast majority of younger clients are fully familiar with the way these devices operate, how they can be added to and how their settings can be easily updated.

Since these devices have also become an integral part of most young peoples' lives - indeed, for some they are akin to an extra limb - the digital hypnotherapy metaphor is instantly understood, and the client feels completely at ease and at home with the entire visualisation process.

Many younger people regard their phone as their most valuable possession, turning to it for communication, entertainment, learning and solace. They already regard these devices as a reliable avenue out of their frustrations, a refuge from their difficulties, a place to find answers and solutions.

Happily, the approach offered in this volume also works just as well with those who are well-read thus providing a methodology appropriate for anyone who understands how to manage a smart-phone or tablet.

Seven full example scripts are presented within this volume, each dealing with a specific problem or ailment. The scripts are infinitely adaptable. The general idea of digital hypnotherapy by way of virtual apps should work with almost any problem and there is sufficient material within this volume for anyone to create their own personalised 'digital hypnotherapy' scripts simply by editing the material they find herein to suit their clients' problems.

The 'Digital Hypnotherapy Modules' chapter breaks the scripts down into their constituent parts, providing a step-by-step methodology for this purpose.

Advice and instructions on how to read or deliver these scripts are also provided along with links to online recordings of examples of speaking to both the self-conscious and unselfconscious minds simultaneously (for an explanation of these terms please see the chapter entitled The Self-conscious Mind and the Unselfconscious Mind) - delivering an overt message to the self-conscious mind along with the more important but covert subtext for the unselfconscious mind to follow, accept, digest and implement.

Speaking to both the self-conscious and unselfconscious minds simultaneously is easier to accomplish than it might at first appear and practice will quickly bring you to competency should you not already be skilled in this art.

The scripts can also be recorded and used for self-hypnosis purposes.

Inductions and deepeners are also provided should you not have your own preferred instances.

Why does Hypnosis Work?

Hypnosis works because hypnotherapists can change reality. The preceding sentence could only make sense were reality to be something other than that which we think it is. The sentence makes perfect sense because reality is very far indeed from what we think it is.

The vast majority of human beings (author included) labour under two onerous misapprehensions which shape and flavour our everyday experience and create our own personal reality. These two misapprehensions are responsible for our beliefs concerning both ourselves and the world in which we (appear to) find ourselves. Against all of the available evidence, each of us seems profoundly convinced that, as human beings, we are no more and no less than, discrete, self-aware, individual, autonomous entities that experience the world of reality directly by way of our physical senses.

And yet what anyone of us regards as objective reality is never any more than a model of reality, could never be any more than a model of reality and the actor which appears within that model of reality and with whom we personally identify could never be any more than a character. This character, our persona, is virtually entirely of our own creation, acting in a play or story which we so very convincingly narrate to ourselves and which takes place inside of our own self-made model of the world.

Almost everyone happily proceeds under the natural yet demonstrably false assumption that the world as we experience it is the world as it is – the assumption being that what we see, hear, smell, taste and touch is what's there. The assumption is natural because we believe we are equipped with sense organs which allow us to do exactly that – to directly perceive our immediate surroundings and our own self within that environment.

And yet, despite our deepest convictions as to the self-evident truth of this, a short investigation as to what is occurring when we believe we perceive anything at all shows that this could not possibly be the case, since, by the very nature of the sense organs used to procure it, all experience must necessarily be subjective, utterly ruling out any possibility of genuine objectivity.

Deepening the misunderstanding as to exactly what it is that is being perceived, the available sense data is then interpreted, compared with personal experience as well as hearsay and then edited and shaped to fit the already existing model of reality we currently hold.

The only experience we could possibly have of this supposedly objective world is subjective in every respect other than in our beliefs. Objective reality is not verifiable in any way whatsoever and so must ever remain a mere inference. Were it to be otherwise then scientific liter-ature would never need to be updated.

Even Newton's supposedly universal laws of motion remain true from a particular perspective only, applying as they do to the macrocosm whilst being completely inapplicable at the quantum level, and so do not, indeed could not, describe the real world objectively as a whole.

Whilst our legislature misses the truth of this completely, our judiciary happily does not as this insight is integral to the proper functioning of our legal system. We are governed by law rather than by principle and the nature of the jury system tacitly accepts that consensus within such a group is the closest we can come to ascertaining whether a certain event took place or did not. The verdict is carefully described to convey the understanding that the person or persons being tried have been found to be either guilty or innocent *in law*, the implication being that what happened *in fact* lies outside the realm of certainty.

Any police officer will tell you that, if after interviewing several witnesses to the same incident, the police officer receives an identical, detailed account multiple times over, then the event being described in the interviews almost certainly didn't happen. Different witnesses experience different perspectives of the same event and will, if they are honest people, give different accounts of what they remember having happened.

Were human beings able to perceive reality directly then there would be no disputes, no arguments and no differing opinions on anything at all. Were the truth of the matter (whichever matter) to be in plain view, then difference of opinion could only come about through either damaged senses, damaged brains or mischief. All disagreement arises out of differing perspectives (different models of reality) being regarded as the truth of the matter by the respective holders of such perspectives.

And, although these ideas may seem rather bizarre to some readers, we have all been quite aware and accepting of them since we were children. Any attempt to deceive is designed to influence and shape another person's model of reality in order to either benefit personally or to avoid censure and punishment. When we lie, all we are doing is seeking to create a particular model of reality which we hope will be accepted as reality itself by the person to whom we are lying. Children learn the truth of this early on and each and every one of us began as a child.

This is clearly evident even in the animal world. Watch a squirrel in the act of burying a nut and, if it happens to notice that you are paying attention to what it is doing, it will pretend to complete its task whilst surreptitiously removing the nut to then go elsewhere to bury its organic treasure out of your sight. The squirrel's aim is to leave you with a model of reality in which the nut is buried in a place other than its true location. Whilst squirrels are rank amateurs, human beings are highly practised performers of this art. How much of what we believe about ourselves and the world in which we think we find ourselves is influenced or intimately shaped in such a way? How could we know?

The closest any of us can get to reality could never be any more than our personal model of reality. Since all models are dependent on belief or conviction - and this is particularly true in the individual's model of their own self with all its perceived strengths and weaknesses - this implies that reality for any supposed individual (for me and for you) is no more and no less than what that individual believes reality to be.

And our understanding of self is no different to our understanding of reality as a whole. Just as the eye cannot see itself and the finger cannot point to itself, the personal self cannot perceive itself. In whichever way I may picture myself it will ever remain a picture and a picture is never that which it portrays. (Frustratingly, however clear and obvious this seems to me in logic, it doesn't seem to stop me doing it in practice).

Yet each and every one of us is so absolutely certain that this is not the case that the issue is almost invariably deemed unworthy of investigation. Hence intractable problems in our understanding of our personal difficulties remain.

Insisting on keeping one's model of the world when all the evidence suggests that one's model is inaccurate results in the types of stress that lead us to seek solutions in drugs (pharmaceutical or otherwise), religion, philosophy and, happily, therapy.

Hypnosis/hypnotherapy works because reality is not what we think it is, not what we have been led to believe it is. What any one of us regards as reality is merely our own, personal model of reality, could only ever be our own, personal model of reality. Each of us does this and it is on this personal model that we base our view and our understanding not only of our individual self and the world in which it appears to appear but also on the relationship between that self and the outside world.* And our view and

---

*The very idea that reality/existence/the world is split into self and other, the inside self and the outside world, distinct and separate, is, in itself, no more than one amongst many models of reality and has by no

understanding of the self, the world and the relationship between the two is what each of us believes to be how things really are. Our view and our understanding of these, our models, are what each of us takes reality to be.

This is borne out by the almost magical effect of hypnotherapy. The client comes to the hypnotist because he or she is unhappy with some aspect of their perceived self in its relationship to the perceived outside world. In the client's experience the hypnotist seems to effect a cure by creating for the client a new sense of identity or a new relationship between the client's view of self and its relationship to the world. In the client's experience a successful trip to the hypnotist results in a changed reality.

In this way, all that is required of the hypnotist is to convincingly suggest to the client that they change their beliefs concerning whichever version of reality they currently take to be the case.

The client believes that they are unable to solve their problem on their own. The client has a particular view about his or her own self, a particular view or understanding of what they take the outside world to be and a particular view about the relationship between the two. The client's view and understanding of their self, the world and the relationship between the two is his or

---

means been universally held across time and culture. The Buddhist notion of anatta/anatman or 'no self' is and has been the central conceptual understanding of millions, to give the most prominent of examples.

her reality - no more and no less. The hypnotherapist aids the client to change their view about reality concerning that self, to change their reality to one where it is absolutely possible to overcome their problem. More directly, the hypnotherapist offers the client a different perspective on reality which is accepted as reality itself. The problem is then overcome because the client believes something different about their reality - the client now believes in a different reality and acquires a different view about his or her own self in relation to that reality.

As human beings we are very much creatures of the credulous variety, shaping our models of the world as much from belief as from experience. When belief takes precedence over experience problems arise in the shape of cognitive dissonance leading to unhappy situations.

The personal problems we have in this world are due to an inappropriate model of what we believe we are and how we believe we relate to this world. The hypnotist is a re-modeller of reality for the client.

The central problem common to all human beings is believing that it is possible not only to see and understand the world as it is (i.e. objectively) but also, crucially, to see ourselves and understand our own individual selves from an objective standpoint. This is no more possible than it is to see our own face directly, and the attempt to do so, underpinned and magnified by our conviction that this is the easiest and most natural thing to do ("Of course it is, I've been doing it all of my life!!!") can lead us into a complex web of mis-understanding and neurosis which, by the very nature of its origin, we find almost impossible to escape by our own means. Having vainly tried all else we eventually make our way to the hypnotist whose skill lies in solving our upsets simply by convincing us, through story, suggestion, metaphor, etc., to exchange our (model of) reality and our understanding of our individual selves (or both) for ones in which our problem does not appear.

> *O wad some Power the giftie gie us*
> *To see oursels as ithers see us!*
> *It wad frae mony a blunder free us,*
> *An' foolish notion:*
> *What airs in dress an' gait wad lea'e us,*
> *An' ev'n devotion!*
>
> **Robert Burns**

Note: All of the above (minus Burns) is, of course, no more than an understanding based on the author's model of reality and no claim is being made here as to 'the truth of the matter'. Whether or not you agree with Single Eye's model of reality, the efficacy of the 'digital hypnotherapy' methodology as presented in this volume remains unaffected. This can be tested within your own model of reality.

The Self-conscious Mind and The Unselfconscious Mind

From a therapeutic perspective, hypnosis is an internally focused state of mind entered intentionally in order to achieve positive behavioural and experiential change. The hypnotic state can be achieved either alone through the process of self-hypnosis or through direction/ guidance/suggestion by way of a hypnotist. In both cases an internal focus is achieved by the person in hypnosis wherein the mind is rendered unselfconscious and therefore open to inquiry, suggestion and change. It is this process which has been shown to be capable of bringing about lasting change in waking conscious experience and ongoing behaviour.

From a scientific perspective, the neural mechanism (that which is believed to be taking place cerebrally during hypnosis) is currently a mystery and will remain so until more light is shed on the relationship between the brain and the mind. There is a further, deeper, problem here in that there is no scientific consensus as to precisely what the mind is or how it works.

In our attempt to understand the relationship between the brain and the mind we find that two very different disciplines are involved - psychology and neural science. Since both of these disciplines are constantly evolving there are currently many theories available from which to choose and to which are continuously being added to.

The human organism is the most complex entity known to us in the entire universe. Conversely, the current ideas regarding the structure and mechanism of the mental element of this astonishing creature are reminiscent, in their crude simplicity, of something made from a child's building blocks.

In hypnotherapy the mind is generally divided into a hierarchy of levels of consciousness. The experiential part of this, the part to which we are privy, the part that believes it makes the decision to pay a visit to the hypnotist or to read this book, is generally called the conscious mind. Underneath this is the aptly named subconscious. Some also term this level the unconscious whilst others regard the unconscious as being below the subconscious. Some believe there are further levels. Some believe that each or all layers of consciousness are divided into parts which may be addressed separately as if they were individual entities. Some hypnotherapists believe there is a basement level to all of this which they call the core.

There is no openly examinable evidence for any of these models of the mind and each quickly displays its shortcomings when searching questions are asked.

Something that does not seem to appear in the existing literature, yet something I continually notice when working with clients, is the fact that when the client moves into a state of hypnosis they have moved from a self-conscious mindset to that of an unselfconscious one - when the client enters the hypnotic state, self-consciousness disappears and the client becomes unselfconscious.

In this way, at least in hypnotherapy, the terms conscious mind and unconscious mind or subconscious mind may be seen to be misleading. Whilst there are clearly parts of the mind of which the self-conscious aspect is unaware, there are no parts of the mind, in my opinion and I believe in my experience, that are 'unconscious' (other than when the client is in deep sleep). I therefore believe it is clearer and more accurate to abandon the terms conscious mind, unconscious mind and subconscious mind and replace these with the terms self-conscious mind and unselfconscious mind respectively.

Is the self of the self-conscious mind the same self as that of the unselfconscious mind? Is the self-conscious mind simply a caricature, a puppet that suffers the whims of the careless, disinterested unselfconscious mind, until the hypnotist intervenes on behalf of that self-conscious mind? Is the unselfconscious mind unaware of self-conscious experience? If so, why should this be the case when the self-conscious mind necessarily remains unaware of unselfconscious experience? If the unselfconscious mind is aware of self-conscious experience then why should it need encouragement to act in order to bring unhappy feeling to an end?

Nobody can really offer universally acceptable answers to these questions, or, if they can, they are either keeping this to themselves, or what they have discovered is simply incommunicable.

The models of the mind as used in hypnotherapy are basic and almost certainly inaccurate due to their elementary nature, but they do seem to provide a useful enough framework for hypnosis to work.

There is another more profound and perhaps unanswerable question that arises when trying to understand the human individual. In the final analysis what is that I really am? What are you? What is this self that is said to have a mind that may or may not be split into various levels of varying awareness of a variety of things? You have (are?) a mind. Your own answers to these questions are as valid as any others.

But, where people are suffering and in need of relief, do these questions really matter? Were clients of a mind that they needed these questions to be answered to their satisfaction before agreeing to undergo hypnotherapy then few sessions would take place. In therapy, we don't need to supply satisfactory answers to these questions. Hypnotherapy works – mainly.

How? I've no idea.

Addressing the Unselfconscious Mind

In hypnotherapy it is understood that beneficial change is brought about by convincingly suggesting to a deeper part of the mind, that alternative ways of seeing, feeling and understanding living experience are not only possible but also more advantageous and therefore in the best interests of the client in both body and mind.

This deeper part of the mind is, in the existing literature, variously called the subconscious or unconscious mind amongst other terms. As outlined in the previous chapter, I believe that these terms conscious mind and unconscious/subconscious mind are inaccurate and misleading and have replaced these with the terms self-conscious mind and unselfconscious mind respectively.

The skill of the hypnotist lies in being able to circumvent the vigilance of the sceptical and critical self-conscious mind in order to directly address the more amenable and suggestible unselfconscious mind.

Through the use of inductions and deepeners, it is possible to divert the generally vigilant self-conscious mind by occupying its attention with imaginary scenes, dreams or ideas and, whilst it is otherwise engaged, talk directly to the unselfconscious mind.

It is also possible to stupefy the self-conscious mind either by shock or confusion which enables the hypnotherapist to communicate one to one with the unselfconscious mind whilst the self-conscious guardian is 'out to lunch', as it were.

It is also possible to address this deeper part of the mind without having to either 'knock out' the self-conscious mind or keep it occupied whilst you communicate with its more important unselfconscious counterpart. This method comprises of engaging in the type of delivery which sounds like ordinary chat but in which direct suggestions or commands are delivered to the unselfconscious without the self-conscious mind being aware that this is happening.

(The chapter entitled, 'Easy for You to Say', includes an example of delivering an overt message to the self-conscious mind whilst simultaneously addressing the unselfconscious mind along with a web link to a recording of this.)

The unselfconscious mind should be addressed with respect and understanding. Try to engender full trust from your client from the moment you meet until you have said goodbye. Whilst hypnosis occurs when the self-conscious mind is otherwise engaged, the unselfconscious mind seems always to be awake, aware and constantly monitoring its surroundings, looking out for danger, in its task of keeping the individual safe. The unselfconscious mind reads body language and interprets intonation. Those with natural compassion for others make for the best hypnotists because their clients' unselfconscious minds trust them from the beginning and are therefore more likely to be amenable to the suggestions you are about to make.

It can be very helpful to spend fifteen minutes or so before the arrival of your client to clear your own mind, remind yourself why you are doing what you're doing (hypnotherapy), and generating positive, good feeling. If one of your primary motivations for being in the business is not to help others then hypnotherapy may not be for you - or your potential clients.

Your client's unselfconscious mind will pick up on your state of mind. If your mind is elsewhere your chances of success are significantly diminished.

If you feel nervous then this will also be picked up on. You can calm yourself significantly by reading one of the inductions in this volume to yourself. If you go too far and lead yourself into trance you will be awakened by the doorbell when your client arrives.

Once you have gained the trust of both the self-conscious and the unselfconscious mind(s) of your client, hypnotherapy can begin.

The Use of Scripts in Hypnotherapy

The worth of hypnotherapy scripts does not lie in simply reading them out to the client in a 'one size fits all' manner. Whilst some degree of success may be found by this inelegant method, the results are very likely to be patchy and disappointing and there is also the possibility of the client being turned away from hypnosis as a possible solution to their problem.

If you are reading a script to a client you will not be able to monitor their skin tone, their rate of breathing or whether or not rapid eye movement is occurring should their eyes be closed. A fully successful hypnotherapy session generally requires constant monitoring of the client's reactions to your words and suggestions.

There is little point in moving on to the main content of your session if the client is not in hypnosis. Some clients will slip into trance and hypnosis very easily whilst others may need more than one deepener to achieve a state of mind open to the hypnotic suggestions you intend to make. You will only know when this has occurred by attending closely to your client's progress. If your eyes are on a piece of paper or laptop screen there is a good chance that you may miss these vital signs.

The best approach in using these scripts in order to get the most out of them is to read them to yourself several times over, learn their structure, become familiar with the methodology and then, after having interviewed your client, spontaneously weave and deliver a personal, client-oriented session from there.

Indeed, all scripts, no matter their origin, work best when moulded around the client's particular psychology and idiom and should incorporate specific information gleaned from the client in your pre-hypnosis interview. This is the art of the hypnotist and it is worth learning as it will greatly increase your success rate.

Digital Hypnotherapy Script Structure

Once the client has been led into hypnosis, a simple scene is painted comprising a room with a chair and a desk. On the desk a device is found which looks and functions much like a contemporary [2022] smart-phone. The client is invited to pick up and inspect the device. The device becomes active automatically and the client is informed that this has happened because the device belongs to them and has recognised them.

The client learns that this is their 'inner controls' device, and that it works exactly like their own phone but with one major difference. The difference being that the apps that they find on the device control the client's own inner workings, and that updating the settings on one or several of these apps is sufficient to solve the personal problem they are presenting.

The client finds the app in question (e.g., the 'Eating' app for weight issues, the 'Phobias' app for particular fears, the 'Psyche' app for emotional problems, etc.).

The client is then encouraged to update the various settings of the app in question, in the same way that they are used to doing when updating the settings on one of their smart-phone or tablet apps, and then informed that because of what they have just done their problem is now either solved or significantly alleviated.

The client's unselfconscious mind can then be directly addressed and petitioned to kindly implement the changes that have been suggested.

Within both provided exductions (Wake Up! and Go to Sleep…) further hypnotic suggestions are detailed.

Easy for You to Say…

The following is an example of speaking to both the self-conscious and unselfconscious minds simultaneously - delivering an overt message to the self-conscious mind as well as the more important subtext for the unselfconscious mind to follow, digest and implement. Words in bold are intended to be delivered in a lowered tone. These will be interpreted by the unselfconscious mind as direct suggestions/commands.

And you may well be thinking, "Well, it's easy for you to say, "**you can do it**," but it's not so easy for me to put into practice", but, I would reply to that, that, the funny thing is that, I'm not just saying it, I'm not just saying, **you can do it**, because, if I were *just* saying, **you can do it**, then, yes, that simply wouldn't be enough, but, as I said, I'm not just saying, **you can do it**, you see, you're also listening to me saying, **you can do it**, which means, you're also hearing me say, **you can do it**, and so, indeed, at a very deep level, below the level of consciousness, **you fully accept that you can do it**, have fully accepted that, **you really can do it**, and, **the next time that you try to do it you *will* do it**, and then you'll look back and think, well goodness me, he wasn't just saying, **you can do it, because you can do it is the case!**

To put it another way, I'm not just throwing the ball. You're also catching it - you have caught it. **You've caught the "Yes, I can" ball** and so now you can **replace your old "No, I can't ball" with this new "Yes, I can" one.**

And yes, **it really is as easy as that!**

A recording of this short piece is available to listen to at www.hypnosis.scot

Inductions

These inductions are included because they have been successfully used along with these particular scripts but should not be seen as integral to the 'Digital Hypnotherapy' approach and other, preferred inductions will work just as well.

As with all the hypnotherapy scripts in this volume, words in bold are direct suggestions to the unselfconscious mind and are intended to be delivered in a lowered tone. Commas are intended to be delivered as pauses.

Apparent grammatical errors, non sequiturs and assorted oddities are intentional.

Please visit **www.hypnosis.scot** for example recordings of (how to read) hypnotherapy scripts.

You Are Breathing

I'd like you now to close your eyes and just notice the fact that, you are breathing. Breathing, is one of those things that you are so, very good at that you can do it perfectly when, **you are sleeping,** without even having to think about it or even be aware that, **this is happening**, which, is really rather reassuring, as I'm sure, **you agree.** Breathing, is one of those things that you are so used to doing that you rarely even notice that, **this is happening,** even during your waking hours. And yet breathing is the key to so many wonderfully trance formative states of mind. A key you've had in your possession all of your life, perhaps without even knowing that it was a key and remaining unaware of all of the treasures, your own, personal, hidden treasures, that this key is capable of unlocking, inner treasures of which you've been unaware, treasures that you've always had within you that merely need to be reached out to and grasped.

And, just simply being aware of the breath, as it flows, is the secret route to your other mind, your deeper mind, that state of mind in which, **you have the capacity to solve all of your problems automatically.** And practice with this will, **produce your key** and allow you to, **use your key to unlock all of your treasures.**

Breathing is the certain method, the reliable route, always to hand, always available, allowing easy entry into a much **deeper** state of mind, a state of mind where personal transformation is possible for everyone, because, simply focussing on your breath, allows you to, **gently open the gateway to the deeper parts of your** being, what we may call your other mind, your quiet mind, a state of mind wherein all things are taken care of, where new habits take form, because, in this state of mind, **you can feel so very differently about things**.

And why should this be the case? Well, you have, of course, been breathing since very shortly after you were born, and, you will carry on breathing for the rest of your life, but the key to a truly relaxed state of mind, the entrance way to the place where, **change is possible**, is the present breath, this breath.

Simply being aware of the flow of your life breath, the easy feeling that comes from just being conscious of being alive by watching the breath as it flows, following *this* breath, flowing in, and flowing out at its own, natural, pace, following the natural rhythm of the universe itself, not trying to hurry it up or trying to, **slow your breathing down**, just simply being aware of this happening, now, merely focusing on the breath, brings about a state of calm relaxation in the most turbulent of situations.

And so, if you would, for me now, please just take, five **deep** breaths, one after the other, holding each one for just as long as, **this is comfortable,** for you to do so, letting out each breath just as soon as, **you would like to**. And you can do that in your own time while I continue to talk and you, **continue to focus,** on what I have to say. That's right, good.

And you can do this anytime that you would like to, **enter a calmer state**, any time that you would like to, **enter a deeper state of mind,** a state of simple serenity wherein the body can, **relax effortlessly**. This is a natural state, you find, where you happily notice that, **stress is already beginning to dissolve away, now**, where **all remaining tension just, melts away, now**.

And so, we shall follow this breath, focus on this breath, and, as you do, you notice that, when you simply, attend to the breath, not trying to influence it in any way whatsoever, simply witnessing the flow, your breathing automatically becomes slower now, **becoming calmer now**, **deeper now**, bringing with it a sense of ever more profound relaxation, an all-encompassing relaxation, a wonderful feeling, a delightful feeling, where you notice, now, that this feeling of ever deepening relaxation has a certain colour to it and a certain scent to it, and as you, **see that comforting colour now**, as a small spark, glowing, radiating warm sparkling light from the very centre of your being, and, you notice the delicate nature of that particular aroma, your senses themselves becoming softer, finer, your mind gladly slipping, now, into that receptive state where, **what I ask you to imagine becomes**.

You see that tiny spark of colour, the colour of comfort, glowing and radiating from the very centre of your being, now beginning to grow now and become ever larger now. That wonderful colour is beginning to fill up the whole of your being.

The colour expanding so much now that it passes beyond the bounds of your skin, and you find yourself surrounded by it, almost as if you are inside a huge bubble of that colour, and the bigger the bubble becomes, the better it feels, and the better it feels the **deeper you**

can go into this, deeper, quieter, softer, so good, yes, that's right. A wonderful feeling, allowing you to focus intently on what I have to say without needing to be bothered by the outside world at all.

And, in this delicious state, it is so easy to **drift off into a world of imagination** wherein **the words you hear become fascinating,** and so I'd like you to get ready to, **imagine the following**…

Your Own Face

I'd like you now to close your eyes and focus on my voice, listening only to my voice as you become aware of the gentle rhythm of your breathing, that's right, following your breath whilst listening to my voice taking you down into a dream-like comfort, knowing that there is nothing that you need to do other than, listen to these words, focus on these words, and follow, each breath, as it flows, in, and out, that's right. And, with each breath you notice that, **your eyes are beginning to feel sleepy**, and your breathing, now, becoming so much more relaxed as you simply listen to my voice, that's right. Breathing deeply now…

And you open your eyes for a second, and see my smiling face and, you know that, all is well. And so, you can now close your eyes again and, **sink even more deeply** than you were before, further down into warm dreamy, easy, gentle, comfort feeling.

Feeling the muscles around your sleepy eyes releasing, all tension dissolving, drifting away, disappearing, that's right. And, as the little muscles around your eyes, loosen, this encourages all of the tiny muscles around your nose and mouth and chin to loosen too.

And, just as an aside, did you ever notice that, you've never ever seen, the thing, with which, you think, you're most familiar - you've never ever seen your own face? Ever! No! Look, you've seen reflections of your face and pictures, photographs of your face, and, most likely, you've seen videos of your face, as well, *but*, a reflection of your face, is not your face, and a photograph of your face, is not your face, and so, the fact of the matter remains, none of these, no not *one* of these, *other* things, could, *ever, be* your face, which inevitably means that,

> Beyond the shadow, of a shadow of doubt,
> As logic dictates, it must be,
> As surely as it's always now,
> In each and every case,
>
> You've never, ever, ever,
> ever, ever, ever,
> Seen, your, own, face.

Fascinating that, isn't it? So much so, you simply, **slip within this, sleep!**

Your focus, **on the inside now**, feeling profound peace flooding through you, a wonderful peace, a welcome peace, attractive, appealing, inviting you now to, **go into that peace, become that peace,** so good, you can, **go so much deeper**, now, and now, with every word you hear me say, each and every one, you, go twice as deep, double-y deep, as deep, as deeper as deepest…

Deepeners

A Bell Rings Behind You

'A Bell Rings Behind You' comprises a list of sensations incorporating sight, sound, smell and touch.

Please insert a pause of around three seconds between each sensation.

I'd like you now to see, feel, smell, taste, touch and fully experience the following sensations:

The sound of a single bird singing in a vast wood.

A blue ship

Seven strands of spaghetti

Fingers and thumbs

Rabbits with tails

An unlikely event

Seashore shells

A glass on a shelf, half full

Velvet

Bare feet on a sandy beach

Eating apples

Receiving good news

One sock

The other one

Baskets of flowers

Laughter

Two cats with green collars

Nursery Rhymes

The smell of lemons

Chocolate string

Loud pink

A bell rings behind you

Tantalising softness

A lighthouse shining in the dark

Landing after a long journey

Finishing work

Washing your hands in warm soapy water

Honey

Giggling

Frosty mornings

Warm, comfortable shoes

Finding keys

Stopping self-harm

Doing the right thing

Doing the left thing

Quiet afternoons

A gentle breeze upon the skin

Forgetfulness

Returning to safety

Seeing the solution

Self-acceptance

Reorganisation

Feeling differently about it all

Feeling that change is possible now

Knowing the time is now

Inner negotiation

Inner cooperation

A return to stability

Deep calm

Quiet optimism

Glad memories

Exchanging thoughts for feelings

A welcome change

Noticing that it **is** manageable

Noticing that nothing is needed now

Tying up loose ends

A new perspective

Feeling *so* well

Letting go

Stresses dissolving

Putting it all down at last

Deep satisfaction

Falling asleep

Finding the path

A gentle descent

Inwards

Downwards

Towards

A deeper peace

Deeper than before and so soft, so quiet

So… blissful

An easy delight

Seeing that all is well

Laughing at one's own silliness

Rest

Forgiveness - total and absolute forgiveness

Trust and belief in yourself… returning

Seeing things differently

And, because of this

Feeling differently about things

And, because of this

Space to manoeuvre

Realising that you can

Solve problems unconsciously now

Awakening sleeping abilities

Seeing clearly that your box of reasons for continued upset can be emptied now

Enormous relief

Seeing that the box is no longer needed

Seeing clearly that your future is full of possibilities, now

Noticing huge reserves of energy are always yours

Connecting with these, now

Confidence, resilience and stamina

A comfort not felt since childhood

Comfort, deep, deep comfort

Going deeper now

Towards your centre

Going deeper than you've ever allowed yourself to go before

Seeing that bright light deeper within

Moving towards this

Brighter, deeper, ever inwards

Until you find yourself

Open, now, to change…

Triple Dream Sequence

Log cabin home

I'd like you now to close your eyes and imagine that it's a long time ago, and you are sitting comfortably in a snug and cozy log cabin, deep in the woods on a mountain in Alaska. It's snowing outside but it feels wonderful here in this log cabin and you are warmer still because you are sitting in front of roaring wooden fire. You've just had a delicious dinner, and there's nothing for you to do other than to gaze into the flickering flames, as you notice shapes come into being briefly before disappearing and appearing again as something else, listening to the crackling wood, smelling that delightful aroma of charcoal and pinewood. And you reflect upon the fact that you are warm and well fed and you have enough supplies to last you through the winter and that there's nothing at all to be concerned about and so in your warmth and in your safety you begin to feel that familiar feeling of deep sleep coming on. Your eyelids are becoming heavy, they close, just like yours are now, but you can still see the glow of the fire through your eyelids, so bright are the flames and you can feel the generous glorious warmth and you feel so comfortable you allow yourself to, simply, **let go**, and you**, begin to dream**…

On the train

You dream that you are sitting on a train in an almost empty carriage, those few other people here in the carriage with you are all occupied with their phones or with books or just simply looking out of the window. You too look out of the window, slipping into your own private world as you watch the beautiful countryside roll by, the train moving quickly through this landscape. You have been on this particular journey before, but it was so long ago that it seems almost new. And yet, as the train begins to climb this gentle hill, you remember that, beyond this particular rise, lies the sea and you know that soon, very soon, as the train tops the crest of the incline, you will be able to see the glint of the sun on the waves of the rolling ocean, and now, happily confirming your own expectations, the train reaches the highest point, allowing you to revisit your memories. You smile a smile of contentment, yawn, stretch your arms and, **drift off into slumber**…

At the beach

And you find yourself, now, dreaming that you are walking barefoot on sand, on a beautiful beach, along the water's edge, as the sun's rays stream down upon you and you take in the beauty of the day knowing that there is nothing, but nothing at all for you to do. You feel the sand between your toes as you walk, taking you back to easier times, untroubled, unpressured, unrestricted, open, free. And so, you begin to, **let go**, begin to, **slip into a world of blissful comfort,** in the overwhelming wonder of this moment, as you feel, now, all remaining tensions simply, evaporate, unable to remain within this quite delightful scene. And, as you walk, you notice that, curiously, your breathing is in rhythm with the waves. As you breathe in, the waves roll in to the shore and, as you breathe out, the waves return. You stop to watch this and the experience is wonderful. You, **become fascinated by this**, your entire being softens and you, **become open to change**…

Blackboard Portal

In a moment I'm going to ask you to imagine that you are standing in an old-fashioned classroom. It's a midsummer's afternoon, and the room is pleasantly warm. You are the teacher here, but all of your pupils have gone home, and you are, now, relievedly, alone. A long, hard day has come to its end and, **you feel tired but happy and content**. Happy and content with a day's work, *well done. That's right...*

It's now time to go home for you too. But there is one last thing that needs done before you do. There's an old-fashioned blackboard on one wall and on the shelf beside it you see a chalk duster and a box of coloured chalks.

The blackboard itself is almost completely covered in words and figures and diagrams, written and drawn in various, differently coloured chalks - still there, from the last lesson, and you know that it is this blackboard, your blackboard, that must be cleaned before you can finally go. Your blackboard needs emptied of all its colourful chalky marks.

And so, you walk across to the blackboard and you reach **down** and take hold of the duster, you see sitting there, next to the box of coloured chalks, and you begin to clean off these chalk marks with long, slow, sweeping movements of your hand and arm. It's a curiously satisfying experience as your hand moves in gentle arcs across the board gradually removing the words, eliminating the figures, wiping away the diagrams and the images, bringing with it, in this steady calm, sweeping motion of your hand and arm, a **deeper** sense of peace and of... **deepening relaxation**.

And, as you continue to clean away these words and figures from the blackboard you begin to feel your own mind clearing in the same way, emptying of all remaining chatter, the thoughts and concerns of earlier, **quietening now**, leaving only, a growing silence, a peaceful silence, a welcoming, comforting, soothing silence as your mind becomes so, **quiet**, so **calm**, so **wonderfully still**, you feel a little floaty and otherworldly, in this deep, warm, comforting silence. Real time seems to have stopped.

And, as you, **experience this now**, as you continue to sweep these chalk marks into oblivion, you notice, in the midsummer's afternoon light, thousands, millions, *billions*, perhaps, of microscopic flecks of differently coloured chalk, scattering, dancing, floating in the air and you see each one of them *light up* for a second, caught, at just the right angle in the late afternoon Summer sunbeams as they **descend** slowly to the floor... a micro fireworks display performed in front of your delighted eyes.

Your arm movements becoming automatic now, so natural, so easy that it seems, **you no longer need to even concentrate on your task**, the board becoming ever blacker, and, as you, **see this**, you notice too, your mind, also, becoming still, emptying just like the board, all inner chatter coming to an end, quietening completely now as you wipe each and every remaining chalk mark away... until all is clear, all is blank, all is empty and free.

And now the blackboard is completely clear, your mind, reflecting this, **now**, also, **clear**, **calm**, **peaceful**, any remaining stresses brushed away, any remaining tensions floating **down** to the floor, in this late afternoon's summer sunlight. And, as you gaze contentedly at the blank, black board, your eyes change focus and all of the remaining tiny flecks of chalk swirling between you and the board become, in this dream-like state, multiple stars, clusters of galaxies, the entire universe forming in front of you, a final flurry of activity before fading as they all gently fall, down to **rest** upon the floorboards until nothing, but nothing at all remains.

And, *now*, you stand back from the board and enjoy the beauty its blank state, unmarked and ready, perhaps to, **accept new information, new instruction, new pathways**...

Note for hypnotist: Now that the blackboard is blank any scene can now be drawn there.

Choice of scenes

A: Avenue of trees with path,
B: Beach scene

A: Avenue of trees with path

And, as you stand, *now*, and contemplate the infinite possibilities of what could be, something catches your eye and you notice the that the box of coloured chalks sitting on the shelf next to the blank, black, board in front of you is beginning to shimmer and to sparkle.

You stand back a step and watch in amazement as *all of the differently coloured chalks* magically rise out from the box and begin to float up in front of the board.

The brown chalk draws a series of vertical lines from the middle of the board to the bottom, whilst the green chalk flies about above making contact here and there drawing ovals, filling them in, now the yellow and red chalk fly up together and work in combination swirling around each other, and as they move away together to another spot a butterfly appears where they just were, more chalks rise up from the box and start drawing, dancing around the board, slowly, gradually bringing to life a woodland scene, appearing before you, the remaining blank spaces fast disappearing now as the green chalk fills in the canopy of leaves, the brown chalk rising now busily creating another occupant and soon you see a squirrel smile cheekily at you from behind a branch before dashing to a higher spot, turning and looking at you again, as curious about you as you are about it. The chalks are so busy now, tiny strokes and dots, bringing out detail, filling in spaces. Little birds appear in groups in several places, each bursting into song as soon as each beak is drawn to completion. The tree branches quickly filling up with birds and butterflies now. A young faun gazes nervously at you before disappearing quickly into the undergrowth. And now, there, in the middle of the picture you discern a path being drawn out by the busy chalks, a footpath is emerging, leading through this tall avenue of trees, disappearing into the beyond, intriguing, inviting, attractive, and, as this scene becomes whole, you begin to wonder just where it leads, curiosity building in your mind.

And now the scene is complete, the chalks have stopped their work and are now, in a line, one by one, floating back to the box and returning to their rightful place. You stand now in wonder, gazing deeply into this newly created world on the blackboard in front of you, so real, so vivid, you feel you could walk into it - and so you do...

You take a step forward and feel a tingle run through your entire being as you pass through the surface of the board, as you step into this vision and find yourself on the other side, leaving the old world behind. You feel the warm dust on the path and know that you are barefoot as you begin to walk forward, inwards, through this beautiful avenue of trees, butterflies passing in front and behind you, knowing now, that you are going to the place where, **change is possible, change is easy**...

B: Beach scene

And, as you stand, *now*, and contemplate the infinite possibilities of what could be, something catches your eye and you notice the that the box of coloured chalks sitting on the shelf next to the blank, black, board in front of you is beginning to shimmer and to sparkle.

You stand back a step and watch in amazement as, *all of the differently coloured chalks,* magically rise out from the box and begin to float up in front of the board.

The light brown chalk begins to draw wavy, horizontal lines across the bottom half of the blackboard whilst above this, the blue chalk is drawing similar wavy, horizontal lines across the upper half of the blackboard. And, as the chalks dance and flit about the board, touching here, stroking there, slowly, gradually you begin to recognise a beach scene emerging. The white chalk now creating shells, the yellow chalk describing a circle at the top of this picture, steadily filling it in, allowing the sun to shine brightly over the sea and sand, blue and grey chalks now revealing a porpoise amidst the waves, a boat appears on the horizon as you watch in wonder as the white chalks effortlessly create two, wind filled sails. There are seagulls now, wheeling across this land and seascape, looking for food, the sea glints magically in the sun beams, the waves rolling into the shore - turning - and rolling out again, and so other worldly yet vivid is this scene you can even smell, *now*, that familiar salty aroma of the ocean, you hear, *now*, the seabirds calling. The coloured chalks, slowing down now, have done their work, leaving the board, returning to the box next to the duster, and you gaze deeply now in wonder at this fascinating, vibrant scene.

It looks so inviting, so real you feel you could walk right into it - and so you do…

And, as you feel yourself pass through the surface of the board, you feel a tingle of enchantment flow through your entire form touching each and every cell in your body, signalling to you that you are about to, **enter a deeper realm, a magical place, a place of change and growth**, of new potential, the chance to, **finally deal with an old situation**, to, **feel differently**, so very differently about it, before leaving it behind in order to embark on the newest part of your journey of life. And, as these thoughts pass through your mind, you notice that you can feel sand grains between your toes and you realise that you are now walking barefoot on this beach, feeling the glad warmth of the summer sun, the gentle breeze on your cheeks and a feeling of freedom runs through you, a feeling that holds the promise of new growth and new life, an exciting feeling, anticipating wonderful change and a welcome, deserved release…

'Updating Apps' Modules

Laid out next is a step by step guide to creating your own 'Updating Apps' hypnotherapy session.

If you are using the 'updating apps' methodology with an older client, it can be helpful to ask them if they can show you that they can easily increase and decrease either the volume or the brightness on their device before you enter into the session. This will assure you that your client is sufficiently familiar with the device for the session to be successful. In my experience it's best to avoid doing this with younger clients as to them this is akin to asking them if they can demonstrate to you how to stick out their tongue, clap their hands or engage in some other activity so natural and straightforward as to be unworthy of enquiry.

Percentages as a way of measurement have been left out when describing the various controls because fewer and fewer young people understand what they mean and how they work.

1. Setting the scene
2. Finding the device
3. Explaining the nature of the device
4. Finding the relevant or appropriate 'app'
5. Opening the 'app'
6. Encouraging the client to change the 'app' settings according to the client's needs or desires
7. Explaining and describing the client's new situation/attitude/feelings according to the changes they have just made
8. Backing up the changed 'app' settings to the cloud in order to 'make the changes permanent'
9. Speaking directly to the client's subconscious
10. Exduction

Setting the scene

The client is led into a room within themselves where they find an old-fashioned chair in front of an old-fashioned desk. The scene is irrelevant and can be anywhere you choose, perhaps your client's favourite place which you learned about during the pre-hypnosis interview.

Finding the device

The very modern device is found on the old-fashioned desk. This juxtaposition of something new and modern in an old-fashioned setting represents the younger person finding himself or herself in an old-fashioned world, or the world in which their parents/teachers/authorities grew up. The old-fashioned chair and desk represents the world of the older generation. The device, being modern represents the client's mind. The device works in a way that the client understands and responds easily to the client's desire for change.

Explaining the nature of the device

The client is encouraged to believe that the device contains the controls for their own internal settings, controls with which they are intimately familiar and so already understand fully. The client is encouraged to believe that changes to the 'app' settings will have a corresponding effect on their experience in the 'real' world.

Finding the relevant or appropriate 'app'

In the examples given the icon for the relevant is found in the centre of the screen and an appropriate description of the graphics on the icon (such as a cutlery for the weight loss 'app' icon, a no-smoking sign on the stopping smoking 'app' icon or simply nervous looking emoticon on the confidence 'app' icon). The location isn't important. You may find that encouraging the client to look for the 'app' through various screens, or even encouraging the client to go online and download an appropriate 'app' deepens the hypnotic state and so gains more value.

Opening the 'app'

In the examples given the client is informed that, since the device belongs to them and serves as an integral part of their very being, they need only focus and concentrate on the 'app' icon and simply will it to open and it will comply. This is not crucial - the 'app' could be opened by the more ordinary act of pressing on it – but encouraging the client to focus and concentrate on their task in order to successfully fulfil it serves to deepen the client's involvement in the visualisation.

Once the 'app' has opened on the screen the client's situation/problem/ailment/desire for change is reviewed and related to the 'app' and its settings. The various settings and controls are pointed out and described. These can be sliders, buttons, dials... It's best to keep these as simple as possible as the easier the controls are to describe the easier it will be for the client to visualise them. The controls that are described are directly related to the client's problem/issue/ailment.

At this stage you can, if you wish, inform the client that there is an update available for the 'app', a newer version with more features and controls. An opportunity presents itself here to inform the client that the reason they are having their present difficulty is that they do not have the latest version of the 'app' in question and upgrading it to the latest version will allow them to more easily solve their problem.

Updating the App Settings

The 'app' controls described in the previous section can now be described in further detail. You can now go through the list of controls and suggest to the client that they update each of the 'app' settings according to their particular needs. In the examples provided these are either slider controls exactly like the slider controls on a smart phone or tablet used for increasing and decreasing the volume or brightness, or simple on/off buttons as found on such devices.

The client is then encouraged, using the same method for opening the 'app' described above, to adjust the settings by simply focusing and concentrating on the 'app' controls and willing them to either increase or decrease in amount.

Review After Updating

Once your client has successfully updated the 'app' settings they can be informed that they have now done enough to solve their problem. Their new situation can now be described to them in relation to what they have just done.

Backing up the Updated App Settings

Utilising the client's knowledge about and familiarity with such devices the client is advised to back up the changes they have made to the particular settings of the relevant 'app'. This is a normal part of smartphone/tablet maintenance and will appear natural and sensible and thus further serve to convince the client that the session is real - that real changes have occurred during the session - and that the new settings will now 'stick'.

Addressing the Subconscious

Speaking directly to the client's unselfconscious mind after the app in question has been fully updated and backed up to the cloud is optional and the scripts can be successfully used without having to do this as the scripts are replete with hypnotic commands throughout. Speaking to the unselfconscious mind gives, in my opinion, another layer to the session bringing about a greater chance of success.

For those who do wish to incorporate direct communication with the client's unselfconscious mind it is suggested that you include the following:

> Thanking the client's unselfconscious mind
> for all that they do for the client.

Requesting that the unselfconscious mind kindly accept and implement all of the suggestions made, to recognise the nature of updating settings and thus change the client's experience in the world to one better suited to their current needs.

Asking the unselfconscious mind to practise life or a particular, relevant aspect of life according to the new 'app' settings.

Exduction

Inform the client that in a short time you will count to ten and that as they hear each progressive number the changes they have just made in the settings of the relevant 'app' will become more and more embedded in their mind.

Both 'wake up' and 'go to sleep' exductions are provided with each script in this volume. The 'go to sleep' exductions are supplied should you wish to make a recording for either your client or yourself to listen to before sleeping.

You may have your own favourite exductions which you would prefer to use. Please do use your own if this is the case but the ones provided here contain additional suggestions/commands to the subconscious.

Full 'Updating Apps' Scripts

Seven full scripts are presented here following the modular system outlined in the previous chapter. These scripts can be used as they are or modified to suit your particular purpose and style.

There is more than enough material in each of the scripts for you to edit them down to fit each unique session.

Neuropathic Pain Relief

Fear of Flying

Stopping Smoking

Bladder Control

Stamina Boost for Runners

Increasing Self-Confidence

Weight Loss

Neuropathic Pain

You walk now into the most peaceful room you have ever seen. Just being here brings a deeper, fuller peace. You notice an old fashioned wooden desk and leather armchair in the middle of the room. You walk across and sit down in the armchair. And there, as if waiting for you, sitting on the desk, you see an electronic device similar in appearance to a large smart-phone.

Pick it up, please, and take a good look at it. It feels so comfortable in your hands. There's a reassuring weight to it. The screen lights up as the device becomes active. It has done this automatically because it recognises you. It is responding to you because, **this is your device, this belongs to you**. What you presently hold in your hand is your inner controls device.

You look at the screen. It's large and bright and, much like a phone or a tablet screen, this screen has many app icons on it. It's a big screen, it's a bright screen and it is your screen and all of the apps on this screen are your personal internal apps running on your own personal operating system. These apps control your inner settings, how you live and experience your life and they contain the controls for what makes up your personality; how you feel, what you think, your personal preferences, your habits, your addictions if you have any, what you like, what you don't like, and all of those kinds of personal things you'd expect to find on such a screen.

And, just like all apps, these apps can be configured in different ways according to the wishes of the owner. And, since the apps you see in front of you now are your personal internal apps, you can easily change your experience of this world and, **neutralise your neuropathic pain levels naturally and significantly,** which is so easy to do, **by updating your internal app settings.**

And, since you are doing this today, here in this place, *because* you have been suffering *needlessly* from neuropathic pain, at this point, I'd like to ask your endlessly resourceful unselfconscious mind to, **kindly revisit each and every, thought, symbol, feeling and memory related to your experience of useless neuropathic pain.**

And, whilst your unselfconscious mind is carrying out this task, you can now return your attention to the device in your hand and have a look at one of those apps in particular and, **begin to address your current situation.**

And, whilst I guide you in doing that, I'd like your unselfconscious mind to look within and, **kindly search for, make ready and apply all of the understanding, abilities, strategies and attitudes necessary and appropriate to comprehensively solve this problem of useless neuropathic pain,** which will, **bring this to a permanent end.**

Excellent, now, if you would look again at the screen on your device, please.

Right there in the centre of the screen in front of you, just where you'd expect it to be, you can see a bright icon with a little picture of your face in the middle of it. This is your Pain Control app and this app contains the settings for the different types of pain you can suffer and also the different ways that, **you can eliminate your neuropathic pain**. And you can clearly see that the little picture of yourself is not a smiley emoticon - it's a stressed looking emoticon. But, **you can easily change this**, so let's start to do that now.

Let's open that app now and see which settings, **you can easily change**, to, **clearly see and understand the difference between useful pain and useless pain otherwise known as neuropathic pain**, and, **completely eliminate all of the neuropathic pain you feel**. And, since this is your screen with your apps and, **you are in full control of this process**, all you need to do is concentrate on the app and will it to open for you. And so, if you could do that for me now, please, just focus mentally on the 'Pain Control' app, the bright icon with the little picture of your face in the middle of it and simply will it to open for you. Good, that's right, and your 'Pain Control' app is opening now.

You can now see that the app is open and it fills the whole of the screen and it is shows a range of controls for all of the different things that you feel. It is here that you will be able to make the changes that will enable you to, **eliminate all neuropathic pain, otherwise known as useless pain, completely**.

And the first thing we see is some introductory text about how neuropathic pain arises and how, **you can easily change your internal settings to banish neuropathic pain from your life**.

I'll read out what it says here:

> *Pain is the body's natural alarm system which alerts the sufferer to the fact that there is a problem in or affecting the body that needs to be addressed. In this way pain serves a good and necessary purpose in persuading us to change whichever activity is causing the problem that is generating the pain in question.*

> *This type of pain is useful pain. But there is another type of pain, a pain that serves no purpose whatsoever. This is known as neuropathic pain which is unnecessary pain and, happily,* ***it is possible for you to eliminate this type of unnecessary pain completely***.

> *Neuropathic pain results from damage to the nerve system and manifests within the patient as pain in areas where there has been no physical damage.*

> *The damage to the nervous system can arise for many reasons the two main ones of which are surgical errors and disease. But, whatever the*

cause, the experience is the same. The pain that the sufferer experiences is of no value because of the fact that it is not indicating a real problem within the body.

By changing your internal settings within this Pain Control app you will, **gain control over your neuropathic pain for good.**

Pain control, i.e. the ability to control your neuropathic pain, lies in first being able to, **differentiate between useful pain and useless pain.** *Do this now, by updating the pain control app settings, and, once,* **you can tell these two types of pain apart,** *and this is easy for you to do, you can,* **turn off neuropathic pain completely and at will whenever it arises.**

This app is simple to use and very effective. **Update your internal settings now and turn off all neuropathic pain.**

And the text ends there.

Well, of that of that is very encouraging as it makes it quite clear that, not only are you able to, **differentiate between useful pain and neuropathic pain**, but also that, once, **you can do this**, you can, **turn off your neuropathic pain altogether**. So let's proceed to,

77

change and, **update your internal settings now,** and this will enable you to, **permanently escape from your useless pain right away**.

Look now at the screen and you will see that it is split into two main sections - one section taking up the top half of the screen and the other section taking up the bottom half of the screen. The section at the top shows two different slider controls.

The first of these slider controls is labelled 'Ability to differentiate between useful pain and useless pain'.

And you, **remember that neuropathic pain is useless pain**, so you, **understand what this means**.

The other slider control is labelled 'Neuropathic pain level'.

Both of these slider controls take up the width of the screen with the lowest setting, minimum or zero to the left and maximum or one hundred to the right, just exactly like the volume or the brightness controls work on your phone, controls with which you are very familiar and, therefore, there is no question at all about the fact that, **you will be fully successful in what you are about to do**.

Excellent. All right, look now to the first slider control please. It looks exactly like the volume or brightness slider controls on your phone and it works in precisely the same way but this slider control is labelled 'Ability to differentiate between useful pain and useless pain' and you can clearly see that the slider is set right in the middle at the value of 50 out of one hundred.

So, you can increase your ability to differentiate useful pain from useless pain simply by increasing the current value of 50 all the way to the right until it gets to one hundred which is maximum.

And now, since this is your personal pain control app, running on your own personal operating system that's running on your personal inner controls device, all you need to do is focus and concentrate on the slider control and just will it to move to the right, will it to increase in value to maximum. Focus and concentrate on the Pain Differentiation slider control and move it from where it is in the middle right now all the way to the right to maximum. That's it, you can see it move now, keep it going, that's it, nearly there, a wee bit more, wonderful, you've done it, well done. Now, having done that, you can, clearly and easily differentiate between useful pain and the useless neuropathic pain.

Now that you've done that so successfully you're going to find the next part even easier. Look now, please, if you would to the second slider control, the one underneath the one you've successfully updated, the one labelled 'Neuropathic Pain Level' which indicates just how much useless neuropathic pain you've had to put up with in the past.

As you can see, this slider control is set very high which means that you've been suffering too much unnecessary useless neuropathic pain. You now have the opportunity to reduce your neuropathic pain to zero.

Now, you successfully increased the differentiation control all the way to the right to maximum but this time, you're going to move the slider control for the level of Neuropathic Pain you experience all the way to the left to minimum or zero so that, **you will no longer feel any neuropathic pain whatsoever.**

And again, as I said earlier, since this is your personal pain control app, running on your own personal operating system, so, all you need to do is focus and concentrate on the slider control for Neuropathic Pain Levels, which you can see is set very high to the right, and just will it to move all the way to the left to zero, just will it to decrease in value to the absolute minimum.

Do that for me now, if you would, please, just focus and concentrate on the Pain Differentiation slider control and move it from where it is presently set at a high level all the way to the left to zero. Off you go, you know what to do. Will the slider for the amount of neuropathic pain you feel all the way to the left to zero, that's it, you can see it moving now, excellent, keep it going, all the way, please, nearly there, a wee bit more, brilliant, you've done it.

Now, experience this, because of what you've just done, all of your neuropathic pain has disappeared! How wonderful is that? And you did it yourself by adjusting your own internal settings. So good.

But look, a new message has just appeared at the top of the screen. Let me read it to you. It reads:

An update to the Pain Control app is now available offering a manual override system for use in everyday life.

It then says:

Focus on the words 'Update Pain Control App' to download and install the update.

Well that sounds very useful, let's download that update now and learn about this manual override system that you're being offered. See the colourful button at the top of the screen labelled, 'Update Pain Control App' and just focus and concentrate on that and just will it to open. Do that for me now, if you would, please.

That was quick, well done, you're getting really good at this. And you can see the download progress bar working now as the update is downloading. Another couple of seconds and you'll have it. One, two, that's it downloaded. Now, another few seconds whilst it installs. And that's it successfully installed now. All of the settings disappear and then quickly reappear again one after the other.

And now, as you can see, in the bottom half of the screen there is a new piece of text is evident and an 'On/Off' button has appeared which is currently set at 'Off'.

And the text reads as follows:

81

The Pain Control App has been updated to fit seamlessly with the physical organism which allows you to reduce any newly arising neuropathic pain without having to open the app.

Your earlobes now function as the trigger and signal to your Pain Control app to reduce neuropathic pain.

By turning this control on you will be able to reduce any new neuropathic pain to zero just by tugging gently on either of your earlobes.

Well that is the most amazing improvement, as I'm sure, **you agree**. So, all you need to do now is to turn that colourful button from 'Off' which it's currently set at to 'On' and then, **if ever you feel neuropathic pain in the future you will remember to tug on either of your earlobes and the pain will vanish.**

Ready to turn that switch to on? Ok, you know what to do, you know what you're doing here, simply focus and concentrate on that button and just will it to turn to 'On'. Focus and concentrate and you'll see it change colour and turn to 'On'. That's it, fabulous, you're a star.

You have just made the most miraculous changes to your ability to control and completely turn off your neuropathic pain.

Ok. Now you've made those important changes we need to ensure that those settings don't return to their old values by accident.

And now, lastly, just to ensure that, **your reduced levels of neuropathic pain will remain permanent**, making your life much more bearable, and that even changes to your own personal internal operating system will mean that, **you will always now be in complete control of your neuropathic pain,** you need to turn the last button, the one at the very bottom of the screen, the one labelled 'Backup App Settings to the Cloud', from OFF to ON.

And if you would do that for me now, please. Focus and concentrate on that last button, the one that will ensure that everything will be normal again.

Focus and concentrate on this button for me pleas and turn it to ON, that's it, good, well done, and you can see that turn from off to on and watch the progress bar as everything is uploaded and backed up to the cloud. Everything is now backed up to the cloud.

First class! You've done it. **The change has been made.** You now, **have a full control of your neuropathic pain**, and you've also ensured that this change is permanent by ensuring your backup system has been turned on. You have done so incredibly well and I'm so proud of you.

And now, let's review what you've just successfully done. You've updated your Pain Control App settings so that now you can now easily, **distinguish between useful pain and useless pain or neuropathic pain**. And, since you've updated your neuropathic pain settings and

83

brought them down to the lowest setting possible so that now, **you will no longer feel neuropathic pain,** as you did before.

And the really exciting thing in addition to this is that you have downloaded the latest version of the app which includes the Manual Override System. This means that should you ever start to feel any new neuropathic pain you won't need to go back to the app settings to change them again, because, **should any new neuropathic pain arise again you can neutralise it immediately by tugging on either one of your earlobes**.

More than this, you have backed up all of your new settings to the cloud so that you know that, **a permanent change has now been made**. Superb.

And so, for the next little while, I'd like you to practise this, your new found neuropathic pain-free existence, in every situation you can imagine in life. Get to truly know and like your new identity whilst I speak directly to your subconscious.

I would like now, if I may, to speak directly to your other mind, your deeper mind, your underlying self. Firstly I'd like to thank you for all that you have done to keep CLIENT safe and well for so long.

CLIENT has been suffering terribly from neuropathic pain, the type of pain that is useless and which arises from abnormalities in the system. You know the difference between real, useful pain and useless neuropathic pain. I ask you now to kindly help CLIENT by keeping neuropathic pain signals out of CLIENT'S conscious mind and experience completely.

Should any new neuropathic pain arise, CLIENT will signal to you by way of tugging either of their earlobes and, when you receive that signal, please reduce CLIENT'S neuropathic pain to zero immediately.

I ask each and both of you now to kindly ensure as well and as fully as I know that you can, and I know this, because you have all power here, that, all of these suggestions be embedded deeply into CLIENT'S mind at all levels, including waking consciousness, dreaming and day-dreaming and this will ensure that CLIENT will thrive and survive as is your true desire for CLIENT to do.

I am so very grateful to you for listening to me, for your attention and for your wonderful and necessary co-operation throughout all of this. Without you none of this could be possible. Because of you and your invaluable supportive role, CLIENT has been successfully able to change and that change is now complete and permanent.

Thank you!

Wake up exduction:

In a minute I'm going to count from one to ten, and, as you hear me say each number, your certainty that your situation has turned around will steadily increase and, when I reach the number ten, you will open your eyes and feel and know that your neuropathic pain has now been neutralised completely and permanently, knowing that fundamental and lasting changes have taken place for the better meaning that, just being you is the most wonderful experience. You will be filled with quiet optimism and deeply calm positivity.

Should you ever feel any new neuropathic pain arise you can simply tug on one of your earlobes and the pain will immediately recede.

In a minute I am going to count to ten. As you hear each number you will feel more and more awake and more and more convinced of the success of this session.

When I reach the number 10 you will be fully awake, your clarity of mind will be pristine and you will be filled to the brim with joyful energy, feeling as if you are capable of anything you set your mind to. You will feel this simply because **it is true.**

And, if you ever choose to come to me for hypnotherapy again, you will slip into deeply into full hypnosis gladly and easily, responding especially well to any and all of the suggestions that I make to you.

And so I begin the count…

1 coming up
2 feeling returning
3 consciousness rising
4 optimism beginning to flower
5 beginning to feel awake
6 joyful energy flooding through you
7 overall positivity flowing now
8 beginning to open your eyes
9 opening your eyes
10 fully awake and ready for anything

Go to sleep exduction.

And now, having carried out all of the necessary change, you can trust your unselfconscious mind to accept and permanently put into place all of the suggestions introduced today.

In a moment I am going to count to three and, when you hear the number three, you will fall into a gentle and peaceful sleep and enter the natural sleep cycle and, when you awake, at the time of your choosing, you will feel fresh, confident, optimistic and very happy to be alive and very happy to be you.

But before I start the count I'd like to inform you of something that I didn't tell you before. Because of the changes you have made today you're also going to, **have so much more patience and understanding with the world and all of the people in it than you've ever had before.** Additionally, because of your new found positivity, **you are now much more interested in nutritious food and healthy exercise,** simply because of the fact that, **you feel so much more positive about everything and you want to keep it that way,** and, **feel better and better and better with every day that is given to you.** From now on you will, **sleep deeply and soundly at night feeling refreshed and invigorated with each new day.** Should you ever feel any new neuropathic pain arise you can simply tug on one of your earlobes and the pain will immediately vanish.

Wonderful. You have done so well!

And, if you ever choose to come to me for hypnotherapy again, you will slip into deeply into full hypnosis gladly and easily, responding especially well to any and all of the suggestions that I make to you.

And so, I begin the count…

1… 2… 3…

Fear of Flying

You step over the threshold and into the most delightfully attractive room you could ever imagine. You immediately feel safe and at home here. You look around and notice that, standing in the centre of the room, there is an old fashioned wooden desk and next to it a rather comfortable looking leather arm chair. You go across and take a seat. There, sitting on the desk in front of you, you see an electronic device similar in appearance to a large smart-phone.

Pick it up, please, and take a good look at it. It feels comfortable in your hands. You find it has a reassuring weight to it. The device immediately becomes active and the screen lights up as you hold it in your hand. It has done this automatically for you because it recognises you. It only responds to *your* presence. This belongs to you. What you hold in your hand now is your very own inner controls device.

Your device has a large screen, and, much like your phone screen, this screen has many app icons on it. It's a big screen, it's a bright screen and it is your screen and all of the apps you can now see on this screen are your personal apps running on your own personal operating system. These apps relate to how you live and experience your life and they contain the settings for what makes up your personality; how you feel, what you think, your personal preferences, your hopes, your fears, your contacts and all those kinds of personal things you'd expect to find on such a screen.

And, just like all apps, these apps can be configured in different ways according to the wishes of the owner. And, since the device which you hold in your hand is your personal device and the apps you see on this screen in front of you now are your personal apps you can easily, change your experience in this world and, **regard flying as an interesting and exciting activity**, simply by updating your internal app settings.

And, since you are doing this today, here in this place, *because* you have been suffering *needlessly* from a fear of flying, at this point, I'd like to ask your endlessly resourceful unselfconscious mind to, **kindly revisit each and every, thought, symbol, feeling and memory related to your experience of fear of flying,** that's right.

And, whilst your unselfconscious mind is carrying out this task, you can now return your attention to the device in your hand and have a look at one of those apps in particular and, **change your identity to someone who now like the idea of flying**.

And, whilst I guide you in doing that, I'd like your unselfconscious mind to look within and, **kindly search for, make ready and apply all of the understanding, abilities, strategies and attitudes necessary and appropriate to comprehensively dissolve your fear of flying for ever.**

Excellent, now, if you would look again at the screen on your device, please.

Right there in the centre of the screen in front of you, just where you'd expect it to be, you can now see a bright icon with a little picture of your face in the middle of it. This is your phobias app and this app contains the settings for all of those things that you have been frightened of in the past. And you can clearly see that the little picture of yourself is not a smiley emoticon but that's hardly surprising. But now, since, **you've found the relevant app,** you can easily make some simple adjustments to, **forget all fear of flying,** so let's do just that so that from now on you will see that, **flying is a completely safe way of travelling that is appealing in more ways that one.**

Ok. Let's open that app now and see how easy it is to change your internal settings and then you'll, **be certain that flying in planes is completely safe, straightforward and enjoyable.**

And, since this is your device running your own internal apps, you are in complete control of this process so all you need to do to, **change your feelings about flying from negative to positive permanently,** is to concentrate on the app and just will it to open for you. And so, if you could do that for me now, please, just focus mentally on the phobias app, the little icon with a picture of your face in the middle of it and just will it to open for me. Good, that's right, and your phobias app is opening now. This is good news because, having seen that the app has responded and opened just because you concentrated on it, this means that you will easily be able to change your settings to, **become a happy flyer immediately.**

You can see now that your phobias app is open and it fills the whole of the screen. And the first thing you see on the screen now is an icon with a little picture of an aeroplane on it for fear of flying. **That's the one you were looking for**. Excellent. If you could now focus and concentrate on the icon for 'Fear of Flying' and just will it to open for you now, please. Good, thank you.

As you can see, the screen is split into two sections - top half and bottom half. In the top half of the screen you see can four slider controls which work in exactly the same way as the slider controls on your phone that you use to increase or decrease the brightness or increase and decrease the volume with the maximum setting to the right and the minimum setting to the left. All very easy and straightforward.

The four slider controls you see are labelled as 'Fear of Flying in Small Planes', 'Fear of Flying in Medium Sized Planes', 'Fear of Flying in Large Planes' and 'Fear of Flying in Helicopters' and, as you can see, all four of these slider controls are set very high towards the right near maximum. This is explains clearly why you've been frightened of flying in the past. But that means too that it's also very clear just how easy it is for you to change this so that, **you feel fine about flying in any sort of plane**.

So, I'd like you to do that now. I'd like you to alter your inner settings in such a way that, **from now on you're going to find the idea of flying an appealing, interesting and fun way to travel**, and you're going to do that by moving all four of these slider controls on your personal app to the lowest setting which is zero.

Look now, please, at the slider control at the top of this list, the one labelled 'Fear of Flying in Small Planes'. As you can see, this slider control works in exactly the same way as the brightness or volume slider control on your phone works. Right now it's set at maximum at the right but you can move that now all the way to the left, to zero, so that, **you like the idea of flying in small planes**.

So, if you would for me now, please, just focus and concentrate on slider control for 'Fear of Flying in Small Planes' and just will the slider to move to the left and soon you'll see it beginning to move. Focus and concentrate on that slider control for me now, please, and will it to move to the left towards zero. That's it, you can see it moving now. Well done. Keep it moving. All the way. That's it. Nearly there. Wonderful. You've done it. **You have lost your fear of flying in small planes**, indeed, **now you like the idea of flying in small planes**. How easy was that? Wonderful. Let's keep going.

Look to the next slider control, just underneath the one you've successfully changed, the one labelled as 'Fear of Flying in Medium Sized Planes'. Just like the first slider control, this one is also set far to the right towards maximum. I'd like you to do the same as you successfully did with the slider control for 'Fear of Flying in Small Planes' with this one for 'Fear of Flying in Medium Sized Planes' and move that control all the way to the left until it gets to zero. Focus and concentrate on that slider control for me now, please, and will it to move to the left towards zero. That's it moving to the left now. Well done. Keep it going. All the way. That's it. Nearly there. Wonderful. You've done it. **You have conquered your fear of flying in medium sized planes,** and, this therefore means that, **the idea of flying in medium sized planes appeals to you now**. And so easy! Let's keep up the good work and move on to the next one.

Look now, please, at the slider control underneath the two you've successfully changed, the third one in the list here, labelled as 'Fear of Flying in Large Planes' such as jumbo jets and large airliners like that. Just like the first two slider controls, this one is also set far to the right towards maximum. I'd like you to do the same as you successfully did with the slider controls for 'Fear of Flying in Small Planes' and 'Fear of Flying in Medium Sized Planes' with this one for 'Fear of Flying in Large Planes' and move that control all the way to the left until it gets to zero. Focus and concentrate on that slider control for me now, please, and just will it to move all the way to the left towards zero. That's it moving to the left now. Well done. Keep it going. All the way. That's it. Almost there. Superb. You've done it. **You have completely overcome your old fear of flying in large sized planes now,** and, this therefore means that, **you now find the thought of flying in large planes intriguing, attractive and fun**. And so straightforward! One more update in this section to go.

The fourth and last slider control in this section is labelled 'Fear of Flying in Helicopters'. And, as you can see, this one is also set far too high. It's time to move that slider control all the way to zero too, and, when you've done that, this will mean that, **you have completely and utterly eliminated all fear of flying in any type of plane or helicopter**. You know what to do. You know what you're doing. Will the slider control to move all the way to the left towards zero. Off you go. That's it moving.

You're so good at this now. All the way, please, and you've done it. You've now made the necessary changes to your feelings about flying. And, because of this, **you now feel completely differently about flying.** Your feelings have changed completely. You now, **find the thought, the idea, the feeling and the activity of flying truly appealing. Flying is something you look forward to doing.**

Excellent. You're doing so well. Now, if you would for me, please, look to the bottom half of the screen and you'll see two black icons each with a little picture of an aeroplane on them. The first of the two is labelled 'Initial Reasons for Being Afraid of Flying'. I'd like you now to completely uninstall those 'Initial Reasons for Being afraid of Flying' and get rid of them altogether. To do this all you need to do is to focus and concentrate on that black icon, the one labelled 'Initial Reasons for Being afraid of Flying' and just will it to uninstall. Focus and concentrate on that black icon, please. Feel this deeply. **Uninstall your 'Initial Reasons for Being afraid of Flying'.** Focus, concentrate... wonderful! They're gone. **You have now successfully uninstalled all of your 'Initial Reasons for Being afraid of Flying'.** So good!

Now, the other black icon, the one labelled, 'Ongoing Reasons for Being Afraid of Flying' I'd like you now to, **uninstall your 'Ongoing Reasons for Being Afraid of Flying'** just like **you successfully uninstalled your 'Initial Reasons for Being Afraid of Flying'**. Focus and concentrate on that last black icon, please. Feel this deeply. **Uninstall your 'Ongoing Reasons for Being afraid of Flying'.** Focus, concentrate... wonderful! They're gone. **You have now successfully uninstalled** all of your 'Ongoing Reasons for Being afraid of Flying'. Which means, logically, that, **you no longer have any reason at all to be afraid of flying in any type of plane.** You've made the change. **You are now what is known as a happy flier!**

And now for the last and final part of this process, the last and final part of what you need to do today to ensure that, **you will find flying an appealing prospect for the rest of your life.**

Now your settings have been changed so that, **flying now appeals to you**, you can, **make certain that they don't get changed back again**, accidentally and also ensure that your system settings are fully backed-up to the cloud. Again this is a very straightforward thing to do. Look to the bottom of the screen you and you can clearly see a button labelled as 'Advanced Settings'. And, as you concentrate on that button the contents of the screen now change in front of your eyes and the 'Advanced Settings' controls are now in *your* control. Now concentrate on the checkbox marked '**Turn Fear of Flying off Permanently and backup these settings to the cloud**' Focus and concentrate on this button for me pleas and turn it to ON, that's it, good, well done, and you can see that turn from off to on and watch the progress bar as everything is uploaded and backed up to the cloud. First class! Everything is now backed up to the cloud. **You now no longer have any fear of flying in any type of vehicle and you've made that permanent**. Excellent.

And so now the process is complete. You have changed. You have updated your phobias app and changed your internal settings and, because you have done this, **you are now completely comfortable about the idea of flying in any type of plane.**

What this means is that, as a direct and clear result of the updates you have just made to your internal app settings, **flying is now and will be forever more an appealing, interesting and exciting prospect for you.**

You've also ensured that, **these changes will remain permanent** as you've backed up your new settings to the cloud so that you can't lose your new settings no matter what happens. And you have done all of this by yourself. You now understand that, **you now have much more control over how you feel about things in your life,** than you previously did, **especially flying.**

You've done so well and because you've done so well, **you are now a happy flier for the rest of your life.**
I'd like now to speak to your unselfconscious mind, your other mind, your deeper mind. Firstly I'd like to thank you for all that you have done to keep CLIENT safe and well for so long.

Implementing and reinforcing the suggested changes made today regarding flying is important and correct. CLIENT was under the impression that flying was something to fear. This was no more than misapprehension and so this fear needs to disappear completely for the benefit of CLIENT. Flying is very safe indeed and so now even the thought of flying is a positive one, an interesting one and something to look forward to because flying takes you to your destination more quickly and more safely than any other form of transport. Flying is fun and very grown up.

This is your part. CLIENT'S identity has now changed to that of one who finds flying an appealing way to travel. (Five second pause) CLIENT loves the idea of flying now. (Five second pause) CLIENT wants to fly in a plane when the opportunity arises. (Five second pause) CLIENT is incredibly pleased with this new identity as someone who regards flying in a plane as something to look forward to. Put simply, CLIENT is now a happy flier. Henceforth getting into an aeroplane to make a journey will be as pleasant and enjoyable as getting into any other type of vehicle to make a journey.

I ask all of you now to kindly, ensure as well and as fully as I know that you can, and I know this because you have all power here, that, all of the suggestions you have heard today are now embedded deeply into CLIENT'S mind at all levels, including waking consciousness, dreaming and day-dreaming and this will ensure that CLIENT will thrive and survive, as is your true desire for CLIENT to do.

I am so very grateful to you for listening to me, for your attention and for your wonderful and necessary co-operation throughout all of this. Without you none of this could be possible. Because of you and your invaluable supportive role, CLIENT has been successfully able to change and that change is now complete and permanent.

Thank you!

Wake up exduction:

In a minute I am going to count to ten. As you hear each number you will feel more and more awake, more and more convinced of the success of this session and more and more interested in the idea of flying in a plane.

You have successfully changed and updated your phobia settings, and, because of this and as a direct result of what you have successfully achieved today, you now, feel deeply in all levels of consciousness that flying is a fun way of travel, because, now, it is crystal clear to you that, flying is completely safe, now in the same way that it is for the vast majority of people and that's a truly wonderful thing to have achieved. Well done you"!

When you hear the number 10, but not yet, you will be fully awake, your clarity of mind will be pristine and you will be filled to the brim with joyful energy, feeling as if you are capable of anything you set your mind to. You will know for certain that, you are now a happy flier, and that the thought of a flight on a plane is something you find truly interesting and look forward to experiencing soon. You will feel this simply because, this is true now.

And, if you ever choose to come to me for hypnosis again, you will slip into deep hypnosis gladly and easily, responding especially well to all of the suggestions that I make to you.

And so I begin the count…

1 coming up
2 feeling returning
3 consciousness rising
4 optimism beginning to flower
5 beginning to feel awake
6 joyful energy flooding through you
7 overall positivity flowing now
8 beginning to open your eyes
9 opening your eyes
10 fully awake and ready for anything

Go to sleep exduction:

And now, having carried out all of the necessary change, you can trust your unselfconscious mind to accept and permanently put into place all of the suggestions introduced today. You have successfully changed and updated your phobia settings, and, because of this and as a direct result of what you have successfully achieved today, you now, **feel deeply in all levels of consciousness that flying is a fine way to travel,** because, now, it is crystal clear to you that, **flying is fully safe and truly appealing,** in the same way that it is for the vast majority of people, and that's a truly wonderful thing to have achieved.

In a moment I am going to count to three and, when you hear the number three, you will fall into a gentle and peaceful sleep and enter the natural sleep cycle and, when you awake, at the time of your choosing, your clarity of mind will be pristine and you will be filled to the brim with joyful energy, feeling as if you are capable of anything you set your mind to. You will know for certain that you are now a happy flier and that a flight on a plane is something you find truly interesting and look forward to experiencing soon. You will feel this simply because, **it is true.**

1… 2… 3…

Stopping Smoking

You step through the doorway into the most beautiful room you have ever seen. In the very centre of the room stands an old fashioned wooden desk and an old fashioned, padded armchair. You walk across and sit down. The chair feels dreamily comfortable. On the desk you see an electronic device similar in appearance to a large smart-phone.

You are curious. You pick it up to get a better look at it. It feels comfortable and just right in your hand and has a certain reassuring weight to it. The screen lights up and becomes active immediately as you hold it in your hand. It has done this automatically because it recognises you. **This is yours. This device belongs to you.** What you hold in your hand now, what you recognise that you are holding now, is your very own inner controls device. **And it feels good.**

You look at the screen and, much like a phone or a tablet screen, you see that this screen displays a number of apps. It's a big screen, a bright screen and it is your screen and all of the apps on this screen are your personal internal apps running on your own personal operating system. These apps control your inner workings concerning how you live and experience your life and they contain the settings for what makes up your personality; how you feel, what you think, your personal preferences, your habits, your addictions, what you like, what you don't like, and all those kinds of personal things that, **you'd expect to find on such a screen.**

And, just like all apps, these apps can be configured in different ways according to the wishes of the owner. And, since the apps you see in front of you now are your apps, **you can easily become a non-smoker permanently**, simply, **by updating your internal app settings.**

And, since you are doing this today, here in this place, *because* you have been suffering *needlessly* from smoking cigarettes, at this point, I'd like to ask your endlessly resourceful unselfconscious mind to, **kindly revisit each and every, thought, symbol, feeling and memory related to your unwanted smoking habit.**

And, whilst your unselfconscious mind is carrying out this task, you can now return your attention to the device in your hand and have a look at one of those apps in particular and, **change your identity to that of a non-smoker today**.

And, whilst I guide you in doing that, I'd like your unselfconscious mind to look within and, **kindly search for, make ready and apply all of the understanding, abilities, strategies and attitudes necessary and appropriate to comprehensively terminate your smoking habit.**

Excellent, now, if you would kindly look again at the screen on your device, please.

Right there in the centre of your screen, just where you'd expect it to be, you see a bright icon with a little picture of your face in the middle of it. This is your habits app and this app contains the settings for all of those things that you habitually do, such as eat, sleep, go to work, take exercise, etc. And you can clearly see that the little picture of yourself has a cigarette in its mouth and the face looks sad and nervous. But, you can easily change this, by making some simple adjustments to the 'habits' app. You can do just that right now so that you will, **see that smoking is an unacceptable habit,** *because,* **smoking no longer has any appeal to you whatsoever.**

Let's open that app now and see how easy it is to change your settings and then you'll, **be certain,** that, **stopping smoking,** contrary to what you've believed, **is easy, straightforward and enjoyable.**

And, since this is your screen, and because all of these apps are your personal apps and, **you are in full control of this process,** all you need to do is simply concentrate on the app and will it to open for you. And so, if you would kindly do that for me now, please. Just focus mentally on the 'Habits' app, the bright icon with the little picture of your face in the middle of it. Good, that's right, and you can see now your 'Habits' app is beginning to open. Excellent. This is a sure and reliable sign that, **you will remain a non-smoker for the rest of your life.**

And, now you can see that your 'Habits' app is fully open and it fills the whole of the screen, presently displaying a range of different slider controls for all of those things which affect your perceived need to do things in a habitual manner, and all of this simply means that, **because you can easily adjust these controls,** to update your internal settings so that, **you can easily change your habits today**, and, **stop your smoking habit permanently**.

You can see that the screen is split into three main sections; one section taking up the top third of the screen another section taking up the middle third of the screen and the remaining section taking up the bottom third of the screen. The top section, as you can see, is labelled 'Eating' and controls what you eat, how much you eat and how much you enjoy what you eat.

The middle section is labelled 'Drinking' and controls what you drink, how much you drink and how much you enjoy the various liquids that you drink.

And now, if you look to the bottom third of the screen you will see that this section is labelled "Other" and this section controls all those things that you put into your body that are not normally classified as either food or drink - things like medicines, vitamins, drugs, amongst others. Let's have a closer look at this section now.

The first thing in the list in the section marked 'Other' is 'Smoking'. Please focus your attention on this part of the screen and just *will* the 'Smoking' controls to expand and fill the screen. Good, that's it, well done. Now you can see that the 'Smoking' controls fill the whole of the screen. You see three slider controls in this section that work in exactly the same way as the brightness or volume slider controls work on your mobile phone.

Now, the three slider controls that you can see are labelled 'Smoking', 'General Anxiety' and 'Overall Contentment'. Each of the three slider controls take up the width of the screen with the lowest setting, minimum or zero out of a possible one hundred, to the left and the highest setting, maximum or one hundred out of a possible 100 to the right-hand side, just like the slider controls work on your mobile phone - minimum to the left, maximum to the right.

The first of these is your 'Smoking' slider control and you can see clearly now that it's set at the midway point. And now, if you look at the slider below that you can see that this one is labelled as 'General Anxiety' and that one is also set at the midway point. And the third and last one in this section is labelled Overall Happiness' and you can see that this one is set in the middle too.

Now, as you can clearly see, All three controls, 'Smoking', 'General anxiety and 'Overall Contentment', have the connected symbol turned on which means that changes made to one of these slider controls automatically affects the other two.

Let's see how this works. I'd like you now to focus on the slider control for 'Smoking'. Focus on this now please and just will the slider control to move to the left which indicates a reduction in your tobacco consumption. That's it. Good. Now, as you can see, when you move the slider control for 'Smoking' to the left, thus reducing the amount of cigarettes you smoke, the other two sliders move as well. As you move the 'Smoking' slider to the left towards zero, the slider control marked 'General Anxiety' also moves to the left, towards zero, at exactly the same rate. You can also clearly see that when the top two sliders move to the left the bottom slider, the one marked 'Overall Contentment' moves to the right. Isn't that interesting? It clearly means that, **the less you smoke, the less anxious you are and the more content you are overall.**

Good, you are now going to, **make some permanent changes here.** I'd like you now to concentrate again on the slider control for 'Smoking', that's it, just focus your attention on the control intently and just will it to move *all* the way to the left until it gets to zero. Focus and concentrate, please. That's right, good, you can see it moving to the left now. And, as you watch that slider control move towards zero, you can see the 'General Anxiety' control slider also move towards zero and you can see the slider control for 'Overall Contentment' increase in value as it moves towards the right. And, because of this, in fact, as a direct result of this, you already, **feel your anxiety levels dropping now,** and a warm, contented feeling beginning to grow within you as your 'Overall Contentment' levels increase. So this is turning out even better than expected. The intention here was to, **reduce your interest in smoking to zero**, and in such an amazingly short time, **you have now successfully done this**, but you've also found that it has had added benefits which you didn't expect: your 'General Anxiety' levels have reduced significantly and your 'Overall Happiness' level has increased hugely. You can, **feel this now**, already and I think you can allow yourself a wee smile for picking all of this up so quickly!

Isn't that a lovely feeling? You're doing so well and I'm sure you can now see that, **stopping smoking is so much** easier to do than you've thought. You have been able to, **reduce the number of cigarettes you smoke to zero,** and simultaneously managed to, **reduce your general anxiety levels to the minimum,** the natural result of which means you will, **be increasingly more content with your life.** And why should this be so? It is so because, **smoking creates anxiety and anxiety reduces your contentment levels.** And, logically, this has to also mean that, **because you have now reduced your interest in smoking to zero, you will,** therefore, **be so much happier overall.** And, since smoking causes anxiety and stopping smoking reduces it, **this is a biological fact.** Simple!

Good, now, just to ensure that, **your tobacco consumption levels will remain at zero from now on,** and also to ensure that, **smoking holds no interest for you any more,** please now activate the 'Hold' switch for the 'Smoking' app', which is the little 'On/Off' button you'll find underneath the three slider controls, **you've just changed.** Again, all you need to do is focus on this switch and will it to turn from Off to On. Do that for me now, please. Focus, concentrate, good, well done. Now, **you feel so much more at ease with yourself,** and so you find that, **your general satisfaction with life rises naturally now.** But the real achievement here is that, **you have eliminated all interest in smoking tobacco permanently.**

Now, all that needs to be done is to look at the 'Advanced Settings' just to ensure that, **you will be completely successful in stopping smoking.**

I'd like you now to concentrate on the 'Advanced Settings' button for your Habits app, the one right at the bottom of the screen. Just focus on the 'Advanced Settings' button and the 'Advanced Settings' screen will open. Do that for me now, please. Focus and concentrate, please. That's it, good and you see the 'Advanced Settings' screen opening now.

Now you can see another four slider controls on the screen. They are labelled 'Feelings about smoking', 'The taste of cigarette smoke', 'Withdrawal symptoms' and 'Meeting your inner needs'.

Look now at the first slider control at the top, the one marked, 'Feelings about Smoking'. This slider control covers how you actually feel about the idea of smoking a cigarette. Look at that slider control now, please, and you can see that it can be set to the right where it is now at 'Desirable' or it can be moved all the way to the left to 'Disgusting' so that, **you feel only deep disgust about the idea of smoking cigarettes**. Concentrate and focus on that slider control now for me now, please, and move it all the way to the left towards 'Disgusting', that's it, you can see it moving to the left now. All the way please, that's it, excellent. Now, because of this, **you regard the thought of smoking even a single cigarette as truly 'Disgusting'**. Just how it should be. Well done. Let's move on to the next part.

The second slider control you can see is marked 'Withdrawal Symptoms'. Look at this now and you can clearly see that this slider control can be moved all the way to the left until it gets to zero. When you do this, **you will experience no withdrawal symptoms from**

stopping smoking. Please focus on that slider control now and begin to move it all the way to the left to zero. That's it. You can see it moving now. Concentrate on this just a little bit more, **this is so important**... Excellent, really, really good, please keep moving your tobacco withdrawal setting all the way to the left towards zero. Keep going, nearly there... Wonderful. You've done it. Your withdrawal experience setting is now at absolute zero and, because of this, as a direct result of what you've just done, **there are no withdrawal symptoms whatsoever from stopping smoking**. This is going *really* well.

Now the third slider control, the one that will mean that, **you just can't stand the taste of cigarettes anymore**. This slider control is just like the others. This slider control is set at a high to the far right of the screen. You can see that it's quite possible to move that slider control all the way to the left so that, **cigarette smoke tastes like burning rubber**. And I'd like you to do that now. You know what you're doing, you know what to do. Focus and concentrate on the tobacco taste slider control and move it all the way to the left so that, **cigarette smoke tastes like burning rubber**. Do that for me now, please. See it move to the left. All the way, please.... Brilliant, and now, **cigarette smoke tastes like burning rubber**. Smoking is now so disgusting and revoltingly horrible that, **you can no longer smoke cigarettes**. You have made a major change and, **this is a change that cannot be undone**. Which clearly means that, **cigarette smoke will always taste like burning rubber**.

Now, the fourth, last and final slider control. This one is labelled 'Meeting your inner needs' and this one is slightly different from the others in that it controls the particular inner needs that you have that you have been trying to meet in the past by smoking cigarettes. If you look at this control now you can see that it can be set to either 'Smoking' or 'Healthy Activities' and that it's presently set on 'Smoking'. This tells us that your smoking has been meeting some of your needs, but, now that, **you've reduced your 'Smoking' to zero,** because, **you are now a happy non-smoker,** we'll need to ensure that, **these needs will be met by other activities** - other activities being positivity, exercise and an increased interest in nutrition. And all you need to do to achieve that is to focus on the 'Inner Needs' slider control and move it from the left where it is now at 'Smoking' all the way to the right to 'Healthy Activities' at the far left which will mean that when you do this, **the needs that you used to meet by smoking cigarettes will now be met by conscious positivity, regular exercise and eating well (but not too much)**. Please do that now. Focus on that slider control for me now, please, and move it all the way from 'Smoking' to the right and set it to 'Healthy Activities'. That's it moving to the right now, good, keep it going, all the way, nearly there, wonderful - well done.

You're doing so well. The next part is fundamental to your task today. I'd like you now to, **uninstall your 'Reasons for Starting Smoking'** and, also, **uninstall your 'Reasons for Continuing to Smoke'**. These, as you can see now, are the two round black icons, one above the other near the bottom of the screen, with the skull and cross-bones on them. Firstly, **uninstall your 'Reasons for Starting Smoking'** because these are

112

clearly no longer needed. Just focus and concentrate on the 'Reasons for Starting Smoking' icon and will it to uninstall and you'll be able to get rid of those reasons completely. If you would uninstall them for me now, please. In a second the icon will just disappear. Just a second, there - well done. **Your 'Reasons for Starting Smoking' have now been uninstalled.** Your 'Reasons for Starting Smoking' are now completely gone and you can tell, **that's a fact,** because the first little black icon has disappeared from your operating system. Now, if you would uninstall the other one for me, please, **uninstall your 'Reasons for Continuing to Smoke'** because, **you no longer have any reason to smoke.** Just focus and concentrate on that remaining black icon for me now please and will it to, **uninstall your 'Reasons for Continuing Smoke'.** Do this now and it will disappear in a second or two. Focus and concentrate, please, that's it, there it goes, gone! Excellent. **You've now completely uninstalled all of your reasons for starting to smoke and all of your reasons for continuing to smoke.** They are completely gone and you are doing brilliantly!

And now for the last and final part of this process, the last and final part of what you need to do today to ensure that, **your days of smoking are now permanently behind you,** and it is now your eternal desire to, **remain a happy non-smoker for the rest of your life.**

Now your settings have been changed so that, **even the thought of smoking is ridiculous to you,** so much so that, the idea of smoking is one of self-harm, you can, **make certain that your new feelings about smoking**

can't get changed back again, accidentally and also ensure that your system settings are fully backed-up to the cloud. Again, **this is a very straightforward thing to do**. Look to the bottom of the screen you and you can clearly see a button labelled as 'Security Settings'. And, as you concentrate on that button the contents of the screen now change in front of your eyes and the 'Security Settings' controls are now in *your* control. Now concentrate on the checkbox marked '**Turn Smoking habit off permanently and backup these settings to the cloud**' Focus and concentrate on this button for me please and turn it to ON, that's it, good, well done, and you can now watch the progress bar as your newly saved settings are uploaded and backed up to the cloud. First class! Everything is now backed up to the cloud. **You now no longer have any interest in smoking,** and, **this is just the way things are now**. Excellent.

Because of what you have done today, because of the changes to your app settings which you have just updated, **you have successfully brought your smoking habit to an end permanently**. And, what's more, you've also ensured that, **there are no withdrawal symptoms because your needs are now being met by your new-found interest in exercise, nutrition and other healthy activities**. And, because you want to keep it this way, **your desire to remain a non-smoker increases daily**. And this is so simply because you have completely and utterly uninstalled all of your reasons for continuing to smoke and you have ensured that, **these new settings cannot be changed back**. Because of this there is just no denying the fact that, you now, **feel completely differently about tobacco and cigarettes**. You now feel very differently about even the thought of smoking because, **the thought of smoking makes you recoil now,** and, **this cannot be changed.**

You just don't want it!

You, **feel differently inside now. Feel now just how differently you feel.** And that's a lovely feeling, isn't it? You want to, **keep that feeling forever.** You fully realise and understand that, **smoking tobacco is something that you despise,** and the truth of the matter is that, **this will always be the case.** And because this is so you can, **feel this now.** This is, **your new feeling about smoking.**

All in all you now, **feel much, much more comfortable within yourself and about yourself.** A, **fundamental change has occurred within you,** and this cannot be undone. You have now taken the required action in order to feel differently about the relationship between you and your old, now abandoned, smoking habit. Now the situation has changed utterly because, **you feel so very differently about smoking now,** and you also feel now that, **you are in complete control of your tobacco consumption rather than the other way around.** Tobacco consumption is now seen, felt and understood for what it actually is, what it really is: revolting, disgusting, filthy, stupid and an utter waste of hard earned money. **Cigarette smoking has ceased permanently,** and, **you are now a convinced and delighted non-smoker.**

And this is just how things naturally are now. Simply this. And so, before you come back to full waking consciousness I'd like you to just feel this new sense of being, confident, happy with yourself as you are and optimistic about anything the future may bring, simply because, **you are now a non-smoker again - but this time permanently**. You are so very, very, very pleased that, **you are now a confirmed non-smoker** and **you want to hold onto that that feeling for the rest of your life**. This is extremely important to you. It is of the utmost importance to you. **Feel the immense depth of that importance now**, feel how absolutely confident you are that this *is* the new feeling, this *is* the new you, because this is just how you feel quite naturally now. A wonderful feeling just like coming home after a long journey and knowing that you are safe, and that everything is in its rightful place. Practise this now, please, in your mind, in all of the situations you can imagine. And I'll give you a minute to do that. I'll be quiet now whilst you practise this wonderful new sense of being happily and contentedly **you** because **you**, **[CLIENT]**, are now a non-smoker.

[Full minute's silence]

Good. Now you won't even seriously contemplate smoking ever again. In fact, **it's so very clear and obvious to you now that the very idea of smoking is ridiculous, stupid and revolting, just like burning rubber**, because, **smoking, now and forever more, tastes like burning rubber and nothing else**. Indeed, because of the changes you have chosen to make today, **smoking is now no longer possible** *because* **it will** always taste of acrid, burning rubber. And what this means is, **you simply cannot smoke anymore.**

I'd like now to speak to your other mind, your deeper mind. Firstly, I'd like to thank you for all that you have done to keep CLIENT safe and well for so long. Implementing and reinforcing the suggested changes made today regarding smoking tobacco will improve CLIENT'S life and allow CLIENT to flourish and prosper.

Kindly accept all of these suggested changes as an integral part of CLIENT'S new outlook and attitude to life. Tobacco smoke is deadly poisonous. Cigarette smoke must, therefore, be kept out of CLIENT'S body. Smoking is now an absolutely forbidden activity in any and all situations. Smoking, as an activity, is now taboo. Taboo. Smoking is now completely and utterly taboo in each and every layer of consciousness. CLIENT no longer wants cigarette smoke in his/her life because CLIENT'S identity is now permanently that of a non-smoker. Since CLIENT'S feelings towards tobacco have changed fundamentally, the smoking of tobacco in any of its forms ceases permanently, now CLIENT has a new life and a new identity as a confirmed and happy non-smoker. This cannot be changed. This cannot be altered. This cannot be broken.

I kindly request of you now, as a crucial part of this change, to completely neutralise any and all nicotine withdrawal symptoms, and instead, allow CLIENT to experience absolute joy and utter delight in his/her new identity as a non-smoker. And so, as this is your part, please permanently increase CLIENT'S interest in and desire to engage in regular exercise and ignite CLIENT'S interest in a good, healthy, nutritious diet.

I ask all of you now to please, ensure as well and as fully as I know that you can, and I know this, because *you have all power here*, that, all of these suggestions are now embedded deeply into CLIENT'S mind at all levels, including waking consciousness, dreaming and day-dreaming and this will ensure that CLIENT will thrive and survive as is your true desire for CLIENT to do.

I am so very grateful to you for listening to me, for your attention and for your wonderful and necessary co-operation throughout all of this. Without you none of this could be possible. Because of you and your invaluable supportive role, CLIENT has been successfully able to change and that change is now complete and permanent.

Thank you!

Wake up exduction:

And now, having carried out all of the necessary change, you can trust your unselfconscious mind to accept and permanently put into place all of the suggestions introduced today.

In a minute I am going to count to ten. When I reach the number ten, but not before, you will open your eyes and notice clearly that you have a vibrant new, optimistic outlook and a peaceful yet joyous heart.

You brought your tobacco consumption to an end by successfully changing and updating your habits app settings, and, because of this and as a direct result of what you have successfully achieved today, you now, feel deeply in all levels of consciousness that, smoking is something for which you now feel complete indifference, because, now, it is crystal clear to you that even the thought of smoking revolts you in the same way that it does for all non-smokers, which is what you are and that's a truly wonderful thing to have achieved.

You are now the same as any other non-smoker because, you yourself are now a non-smoker again, but this time permanently. Smoking is something you regard now as completely unacceptable and ridiculous and this can never change. The very thought of smoking simply disgusts you. You just don't want it. You are certain, and you feel deeply within yourself, at all levels of consciousness that this stopping smoking hypnosis session has been, is, and will continue to be a complete success. Smoking isn't something you do. You don't want to smoke. You have forgotten how, simply because, **you just don't want it**. And that's just how it is.

And, if you ever choose to come to me for hypnotherapy again, you will slip into deep hypnosis gladly and easily, responding especially well to all of the suggestions that I make to you.

And so, I begin the count…

1. Coming up
2. Feeling returning
3. Consciousness rising
4. Optimism beginning to flower
5. Beginning to feel awake
6. Joyful energy flooding through you
7. Overall positivity flowing now
8. Beginning to open your eyes
9. Opening your eyes
10. Fully awake and ready for anything

Go to sleep exduction:

And now, having carried out all of the necessary change, you can trust your unselfconscious mind to accept and permanently put into place all of the suggestions introduced today.

You have brought your tobacco consumption to an end by successfully changing and updating your habits app settings, and, because of this and as a direct result of what you have successfully achieved today, you now, **feel deeply in all levels of consciousness that smoking is something for which you feel complete indifference,** because, now, **it is crystal clear to you that even the thought of smoking is totally revolting** in the same way that it is for all non-smokers and that's a truly wonderful thing to have achieved.

You are now the same as any other non-smoker because, **you yourself are now a non-smoker again, but, this time permanently**. Smoking is something you regard now as completely unacceptable and ridiculous and this can never change. **The very thought of smoking simply disgusts you**. You are certain, and you feel deeply within yourself, at all levels of consciousness that this stopping smoking hypnosis session has been, is, and will continue to be a complete success. **Smoking is not something that you do. Smoking is no longer something that you can do**. You have simply forgotten how to do it because, **now your identity is that of a non-smoker**.

In a moment I am going to count to three and, when you hear the number three, you will fall into a gentle and peaceful sleep and enter the natural sleep cycle and, when you awake, at the time of your choosing, you will feel fresh, confident, optimistic and very happy to be alive and very happy to be you, a convinced non-smoker.

And, if you ever choose to come to me for hypnotherapy again, you will slip into deep hypnosis gladly and easily, responding especially well to all of the suggestions that I make to you.

And so, I begin the count…

1… 2… 3…

Bladder Control

And now the scene changes and you walk into the most beautiful room you have ever seen. In the centre of the room, on a perfectly round antique rug, sits an old fashioned wooden desk and leather armchair. You make your way across the room taking in all of its beauty. You walk towards the desk and chair and you take a seat. And there, on the desk in front of you, you see an electronic device similar in appearance to a large smartphone.

Pick it up, please, and hold it. It feels comfortable in your hands, doesn't it? And it has a balanced, reassuring weight to it. The screen lights up as the device becomes active. It has done this automatically because it recognises you. It is responding to you because, **this is your device**. What you presently hold in your hand is your inner controls device.

As you can see, this device has large bright screen much like a smart phone or tablet screen but bigger. And, much like those types of screen, this screen has many app icons on it. It's a big screen, it's a bright screen and it is your screen and all of the apps on this screen are your personal internal apps running on your own personal operating system. These apps control how you live and experience your life and they contain the settings for what makes up your personality - how you feel, what you think, your personal preferences, your contacts and all those kinds of personal things you'd expect to find on such a screen.

And, since you are doing this today, here in this place, *because* you have been suffering *needlessly* from weak bladder control, at this point, I'd like to ask your endlessly resourceful unselfconscious mind to, **kindly revisit each and every, thought, symbol, feeling and memory related to your experience of weak bladder control,** that's right.

And, whilst your unselfconscious mind is carrying out this task, you can now return your attention to the device in your hand and have a look at one of those apps in particular and, **regain full control over when you feel you need to urinate.**

And, whilst I guide you in doing that, I'd like your unselfconscious mind to look within and, **kindly search for, make ready and apply all of the understanding, abilities, strategies and attitudes necessary and appropriate to regain control over when you feel you need to urinate.**

Excellent, now, if you would look again at the screen on your device, please.

Right there in the centre of the screen in front of you, just where you'd expect it to be, you can see a bright icon with a little picture of you in the middle of it. This is your Bladder Control app and this app allows you to, **regain normal bladder control,** because it contains the all the settings for those things that affect your perceived need to empty your bladder. **You will do this easily**, by making some necessary adjustments to the Bladder Control app, so you're going to exactly that now and a direct result of this will be that you will, **have increased control of your bladder.**

Let's open that app now and see what can be changed in order that, **your bladder is under your control**. And, since this is your screen with your apps and, **you are in full control of this process** all you need to do is simply concentrate on the app and will it to open for you. And so, if you could do that for me now, please, just focus mentally on the 'Bladder Control' app, the bright icon with the little picture of your face in the middle of it. Good, that's right, and your 'Bladder Control' app is opening now. Excellent.

You can now see that the app is fully open and it fills the whole of the screen and displays a range of different slider controls for settings which can, **increase the length of time you can go without needing to empty your bladder**, which means simply that, **you can easily change your internal settings**, as a result of which, **you can wait significantly longer without needing to empty your bladder**.

The screen is split into two main sections - one section in the top half of the screen and the other section in the bottom half of the screen. The top section, as you can see, contains three slider controls which directly affect your need to empty your bladder. These are labelled 'Bladder Elasticity', 'General Anxiety' and 'Perception of Time'. Each of the three slider controls take up the width of the screen with the lowest setting to the left and the highest setting to the right, just like the volume and brightness slider controls on your phone and just as simple and straightforward to adjust.

The first of these is your 'Bladder Elasticity' slider control and you can see clearly now that it's set at a fairly low setting at around 12 out of possible 100. And now, if you look at the slider below that you can see that this one is labelled as 'General Anxiety' and that one is set quite high at around 73 out of a possible 100. And the third and last one in this section is labelled Perception of Time' and you can see that this one is different to the previous two in that it is set right in the middle at exactly 50 out of a possible 100, but this one also has a switch that can be set at either 'Fixed' or 'Variable' and in brackets it reads, (Dependent on Conditions)'. You can see that the 'Perception of Time' switch is currently set to 'Fixed'.

Now, before you adjust any of these settings let's have a look at the bottom section of the screen and see what you have there.

The section at the bottom also shows three different slider controls and these are controls for things you might be surprised to find in a 'Bladder Control' app. Each of these three slider controls also take up the width of the screen with the lowest setting to the left and the highest setting to the right. The first of these is your 'Self-Acceptance' slider control and you can see clearly now that it's set at a fairly low at around 19 out of a possible 100. And now, if you look at the slider below that you can see that this one is labelled as 'Self-Forgiveness' and that too is set very low at around 23 out of a possible 100. And the third and last slider control in this section is labelled 'Self-Confidence' and you can see that this one is much like the previous two in that it is set fairly low at just under 25 out of a possible 100.

Good, you will adjust those ones later but for the moment please look back to the three settings that you can see in the top half of the screen and start making the required adjustments to those settings.

First off is the 'General Anxiety' control which, as we saw earlier, is set quite high at 73 out of a possible 100. And, as you know, as you are quite aware, anxiety levels can directly affect your need to empty your bladder. Let's, **reduce your anxiety levels permanently now**, by moving the 'General Anxiety' setting all the way down to minimum and, since these settings directly control your inner feelings, once you've minimised the setting you'll, **feel differently, and feel less anxious overall**. And, in the same manner that you opened the app all you need to do now is to focus and concentrate on the 'General Anxiety' app slider control and just will it to slide to the left, immediately reducing your underlying levels of anxiety. Do that for me now, please. Just focus and concentrate on the slider control for 'General Anxiety' and simply will it to move to the left towards minimum. That's it, good. You can see it moving now. Keep it moving to the left, please. And, as you watch the slider control move steadily to the left, **you can feel your anxiety levels dropping now,** as I speak. Isn't that a lovely feeling? You're doing so well and I'm sure you can now see that this is so much simpler to change than you first might have imagined.

Now, just to ensure that, **your general anxiety levels will remain low from now on**, please now activate the 'Hold' switch for the 'General Anxiety' slider control which you can see just to the right of the slider control itself. Again, all you need to do is focus on this 'hold' switch and just will it to turn from Off to On. Focus and concentrate, please. Good, that's it. Well done. **Now your general** anxiety levels are now permanently at a minimum, and you will now find that, **because of this you allow your general satisfaction with life to rise naturally**.

Good, let's move down to the second control slider in the top half of the screen, the one that's labelled 'Bladder Elasticity'. As we saw earlier this one is set quite low at 12 out of a possible 100. Let's now, **increase your 'Bladder Elasticity' to something much more helpful to you**. What this does is, **increase your bladder capacity whenever necessary**. Please focus now on that slider control and move the setting almost all the way along to the right to increase your Bladder Elasticity to the maximum setting. Do this in the same way, **you successfully moved your 'General Anxiety' slider control to the minimum**, but this time you'll move the 'Bladder Elasticity' slider control to the right to the maximum. Focus and concentrate, please, that's right, you can see it moving now, keep it going, that's it, all the way to the right. Wonderful, well done! From now on you'll find that, **you won't need to empty your bladder so often now,** because, **your bladder capacity can stretch according to the situation in which you find yourself.**

Now for the last control in the upper half of the screen, the control slider that's labelled 'Perception of Time'. As we saw earlier this slider control is set exactly in the middle at 50 out of a possible 100. We also saw that the switch for this slider control is set to 'Fixed' rather than 'Variable'. Focus on that switch now, for me, please, and change it from 'Fixed' to 'Variable'. Focus and concentrate as you did before, That's right. That's it, excellent! This means that you'll find from now on that, your perception of time can stretch, just like your bladder, **dependent on the particular situation in which you find yourself.**

You're doing so very well. And this means that the other three slider controls in the bottom half of the screen will prove no difficulty to you at all. Let's have a look at these now.

The three slider controls for your Bladder app that you can see in the bottom half of the screen are labelled 'Self-Acceptance', 'Self-Forgiveness' and 'Self-Confidence'.

The first of these is your 'Self-Acceptance' slider control and as you can see it's set at a fairly low at around 19 out of a possible 100. And now, if you look at the slider below that, the one labelled as 'Self-Forgiveness' you can see that one is also set very low at around 23 out of a possible 100. And the third and last slider control in this section is labelled 'Self-Confidence' and you can see that this one is much like the other two in that it is set fairly low at just under 25 out of a possible 100.

Good. I'd like you to move all of these slider controls, the slider controls for 'Self-Acceptance', 'Self-Forgiveness' and 'Self-Confidence' all the way to maximum, please.

You can start with the first one, the slider control for 'Self-Acceptance'. You know what to do, you know what you're doing. Just focus and concentrate on the slider control for 'Self-Acceptance' and will it to move all the way to the right which will, **increase your feelings of self-acceptance to the maximum**. That's it. That's right and you can see it moving now. Keep it going, all the way, that's right, and you've done it. You now, **fully and happily accept who you are**, and, **be very comfortable with just being you**.

Excellent. Two more to go. Please move your focus now to the next one, the slider control for 'Self-Forgiveness'. Focus and concentrate on moving that slider control to the right all the way to the maximum, please. Good, you're really getting good at this as you can see it moving to the right now. Keep it moving, please. That's it, that's right, keep going, all the way, wonderful, you've done it. And now, **you are able to forgive yourself fully**, and that's a lovely feeling, isn't it? Good.

Now the last slider control. The slider control labelled 'Self-Confidence'. I'd like you to move this slider control to maxim as well, please. Once you do this you'll find that, **you have every reason to feel self-confident**. And, **this will be easy and natural for you**. So, you know what to do. Focus and concentrate on the 'Self-Confidence' slider control and move that one all the way to the right towards maximum, please, focus and concentrate, good, you can see it moving now, well done, keep it moving, all the way, and you've done it. Superb.

And, now, **because you have successfully updated your bladder app settings**, and, **the elasticity of your bladder has increased significantly**, you should now make sure that, **these changes cannot be undone**, and also ensure that your system settings are fully backed-up to the cloud. Again this is a very straightforward thing to do. Look to the bottom of the screen you and you can clearly see a button labelled as '**Make these changes permanent**'. Turn this button on just by focussing and concentrating on it. Do that for me now, please. Focus and concentrate and will the switch to turn from off to on - that's it. Excellent. You've now made all the changes permanent.

Focus and concentrate on this button for me pleas and turn it to ON, that's it, good, well done, and you can see that turn from off to on and watch the progress bar as everything is uploaded and backed up to the cloud. First class! Everything is now backed up to the cloud. **You can now go much longer without needing to empty your bladder and you have made that permanent.** Excellent.

You are so good at this!

And now the process is complete. **You have,** updated your Bladder app settings and, **successfully alleviated your anxiety over this matter.** You've also ensured that, **these changes will remain permanent** because you've backed up all of these changes to the cloud so that, **you cannot lose your new settings no matter what happens.** And you have done all of this yourself. You can now see and feel that, **you now have vastly increased your control over when you need to urinate.** You have done so very well indeed.

You have made some wonderful changes to your internal settings and as a direct result of what you have just done you have regained control over your bladder and thus you now, have increased control over when you need to urinate.

All in all you now, feel much, **much more comfortable within yourself and about yourself**, at all levels. A fundamental change has occurred within you because you have now taken the required action in order to, **feel so very differently about the relationship between you and your bladder**, by updating your internal settings.

All of this has brought about an improved situation for you. Inner peace and calm is now your normal feeling. This new peace that you feel within is truly wonderful and all that you deserve - a deep and lasting peace that will become more established as each day passes which means that, **your feelings of self-consciousness in any social situation are vastly reduced, almost to zero**. Feel that deeply now. Feel just how magical this is. Know that, **this is permanent change,** now and be joyful. And this is just the beginning. Self-confidence is now growing within you and all remaining inner tension is simply evaporating leaving you feeling free and optimistic and full to the brim of delightful energy and enthusiasm about life. You feel so much better all over and through and through and this is simply a normal and consistent part of who you are now.

I'd like you now to practise the happy new relationship you have with your bladder. Practise this now in your mind in all of the situations you can imagine. Imagine being out longer and being confident and comfortable with it. Experience the joy of putting into practice all of the changes you have successfully made today by updating your Bladder Control app settings.

And, whilst you do that I would like to speak directly to your other mind, your deeper mind. I am speaking to your wiser self now.

Firstly, I'd like to thank you for all that you have done to keep CLIENT safe and well for so long. You can do even more for CLIENT simply by kindly implementing and reinforcing the suggested changes made today regarding CLIENT'S bladder.

Allow CLIENT'S bladder elasticity to expand, allow CLIENT'S experience of time to stretch when appropriate and give CLIENT full confidence in being out and about and taking part fully in society again by doing this. Return CLIENT'S bladder and CLIENT'S relationship to his/her bladder to full health and maintain this diligently in an ongoing manner.

Bring a calm and untroubled outlook to CLIENT'S life. Allow CLIENT to sleep fully and deeply and to reconnect with all parts of his/her body.

I ask kindly of you now to please ensure, as well and as fully as I know that you can, and I know this because you have all power here, that all of these suggestions are now embedded deeply into CLIENT'S mind at all levels, including waking consciousness, dreaming and day-dreaming and this will ensure that CLIENT will thrive and survive as is your true desire for CLIENT to do.

I am so very grateful to you for listening to me, for your attention and for your wonderful and necessary co-operation throughout all of this. Without you none of this could be possible. Because of you and your invaluable supportive role, CLIENT has been successfully able to change and that change is now complete and permanent.

Thank you!

Wake up exduction:

In a minute I am going to count to ten. As you hear each number you will feel more and more awake and more and more convinced of the success of this session.

When I reach the number 10, but not yet, you will be fully awake, your clarity of mind will be pristine and you will be filled to the brim with joyful energy, feeling as if you are capable of anything you set your mind to. You will feel this simply because **it is true.**

What is also true is that now you have an improved relationship with your bladder. You feel more confident and accepting of yourself and your bladder elasticity has increased. Because of all of these factors you will be able to go significantly longer without feeling the need to empty your bladder.

And, if you ever choose to come to me for hypnosis again, you will slip into deep hypnosis gladly and easily, responding especially well to any and all of the suggestions that I make to you.

And so I begin the count…

    1 coming up
    2 feeling returning
    3 consciousness rising
    4 optimism beginning to flower
    5 beginning to feel awake

6 joyful energy flooding through you
7 overall positivity flowing now
8 beginning to open your eyes
9 opening your eyes
10 fully awake and ready for anything

Go to sleep exduction:

And now, having carried out all of the necessary change, you can trust your unselfconscious mind to, **accept and permanently put into place all of the suggestions introduced today**. Life for you has become so much more manageable and I can tell you this simply because, **this is true**.

What is also true is that now you have an improved relationship with your bladder. You feel more confident and accepting of yourself and your bladder elasticity has increased. Because of all of these factors you will be able to go significantly longer without feeling the need to empty your bladder.

In a moment I am going to count to three and, when you hear the number three, you will fall into a gentle and peaceful sleep and enter the natural sleep cycle and, when you awake, at the time of your choosing, you will feel fresh, confident, optimistic and very happy to be alive and very happy to be you

1... 2... 3...

Stamina (Running)

You step out into a rather futuristic looking room in the centre of which you see an old-fashioned wooden desk and a comfortable looking armchair. You walk over to this desk and sit down. The chair is wonderfully comfortable, which is unsurprising as this chair was made for you. And there, sitting waiting for your attention on the desk, you see an electronic device similar in appearance to a large smart-phone.

You are intrigued. Pick it up to look at it. It feels comfortable in your hands and it has a pleasant, reassuring weight to it, doesn't it? The screen lights up and the device becomes active as you hold it in your hand. It has done this automatically because it recognises you. **This is your device. This belongs to you**. What you hold in your hand now is your inner controls device.

The screen is large and bright and, much like a phone or a tablet screen, this screen has many apps on it. It's a big screen, it's a bright screen and it is your screen and all of the apps on this screen are your personal internal apps running on your own personal operating system. These apps control your inner workings, how you live and experience your life. These apps contain the settings for what makes up your personality - how you feel, what you think, your personal preferences, your habits, your addictions, should you have any, what you like, what you don't like, your stamina levels and all of those kinds of personal things you'd expect to find on such a screen.

And, just like all apps, these apps can be configured in different ways according to the wishes of the owner. And, since the device which you hold in your hand is yours and the apps you see on this screen in front of you now are your apps you can easily, change your experience in this world and, **increase your stamina levels naturally and significantly,** simply by updating your internal app settings.

And, since you are doing this today, here in this place, *because* you have been suffering *needlessly* from having insufficient stamina, at this point, I'd like to ask your endlessly resourceful unselfconscious mind and, **kindly revisit each and every, thought, symbol, feeling and memory related to your experience of having insufficient stamina,** that's right.

And, whilst your unselfconscious mind is carrying out this task, you can now return your attention to the device in your hand and have a look at one of those apps in particular and, **subconsciously increase your stamina levels when you are running..**

And, whilst I guide you in doing that, I'd like your unselfconscious mind to look within and, **kindly search for, make ready and apply all of the understanding, abilities, strategies and attitudes necessary and appropriate to significantly increase your stamina levels.**

Excellent, now, if you would look again at the screen on your device, please.

Right there in the centre of the screen in front of you, just where you'd expect it to be, you can see a bright icon with a little picture of you running on it. This is your Running Stamina app and this app contains the settings for the amount of stamina that is accessible to you when you are running. And you can clearly see that the expression on the face of little picture of yourself is not one of concentrated focus but of a person trying to focus on too many things at once. But, **this is easily changed,** so let's start to do that now so that you will, **have full access to extra stamina when you are running.**

I'd like you to open that app now and see what, **you can easily change**, to, **increase your depth of stamina when you are running,** and so allow you to, **access more stamina when you run**. And, since this is your screen with your apps and, **you are in complete control of this process**, all you need to do is concentrate on the app and just will it to open for you. And so, if you could do that for me now, please, just focus mentally on the 'Stamina' app, the bright, colourful icon with the little picture of you running in the middle of it. Good, that's right, and your 'Running Stamina' app is opening now and filling up the entire screen.

The first thing can see, now your Stamina app is open, is some introductory text explaining exactly how stamina works and how, **you can increase your stamina just by updating your Stamina app settings**, which I shall read out for you now.

Your quantum of stamina is directly affected by several factors all of which lie within the controls of this app. This app was designed by collating and processing the information gathered by interviewing today's most successful athletes and using that information to allow everyone to share in their success by allowing them to change their own internal settings in order to get the maximum out of their reserves of stamina.

STAMINA is built of the seven steps of Strength, Tenacity, Attitude, Mindfulness, Inspiration, Nerve and Achievement.

Human beings in general fail to achieve all that they possibly can because their minds are almost invariably split into many activities simultaneously and their mental focus is therefore lost or significantly reduced. Huge reserves of energy and resilience are wasted due to a simple lack of focus, insufficient self-belief, and a chattering mind which fritters away reserves of energy by constantly reviewing the unchangeable past and fantasising about an unknowable future.

The app has been streamlined in such a way that these three crucial effects can be minimised in order that, **you have the ability to perform at your optimum level.**

Well, all of that seems very clear. Your internal settings need to be changed and you can do that easily by updating your Stamina app settings.

So, let's now look at the controls in the lower section to see what you can do so that you can, **increase the amount of stamina that you can access when running**, after which, **you will climb the seven steps of STAMINA with ease: Strength, Tenacity, Attitude, Mindfulness, Inspiration, Nerve and Achievement.**

The larger section underneath this one shows three different slider controls. All three of these slider controls take up the width of the screen with the lowest setting, zero out of a possible 100 to the left and the highest setting one hundred out of a possible 100 to the right, just exactly like the slider controls you're already familiar with that you use for increasing or decreasing the brightness or the volume on your phone.

The first slider control in this list is labelled 'Internal Focus'. The second slider control is labelled 'Self-belief' and the third control is labelled 'Number of thought threads'.

And so, as is shown in the paragraph at the top of the screen, **you can easily increase the amount of stamina available to you by adjusting these three controls**. And I'd like you to, **do that now**.

Look at the first slider control on this list, the one labelled 'Internal Focus'.

Now, as you can see, your internal focus level can be set at anywhere between 0 out of a possible 100 at the far left to 100 out of a possible 100 at the far right. Right now the slider control for Internal Focus is set at only 53 out of a possible 100 and this tells us that when you've been running your mind has clearly not been fully focussed on the task in hand which would explain why you've been having problems.

And so, I'd like you now to adjust this setting which will, **markedly sharpen your internal focus when running**. To achieve this all that you need to do is to focus on the slider control and simply will it to move to the right towards maximum. Please focus and concentrate now on the Internal Focus slider control now and just will it to move to the right. That's right, just like that, and you can see it moving to the right now, increasing your internal focus levels as it does. I'd like you to move it up to 95 out of a possible 100. Just a wee bit more, that's it. Excellent. Now let's see how what you've just done has affected the main readout at the top of the screen, the readout which tells you how much stamina you have available to you when running. And you can see that it's gone up from 66 out of a possible 100 to 75 out of a possible 100 - which is an increase of 9 out of a possible 100 overall. How easy was that? So good! Because of what you have just achieved, **whenever you run your internal focus will be maximised**.

Ok, let's keep up the good work. Have a look now, if you would, at the second of the three slider controls. The second slider control is labelled 'Self-Belief' and you can see that it's set at only 67 out of a possible 100 when you're running. I'd like you now to move that slider to the right and increase it to 95 out of a possible 100 just like you successfully did with the 'Internal Focus' control. Focus and concentrate on the slider control, please, and just will it to move to the right. Do that for me now, please. That's right, that's it moving now, keep it going all the way to 95 out of a possible 100… Excellent. Well done. Now, take a quick look up at the readout at the top of the screen and you will see that your accessible stamina levels whilst running have been increased by a further 10 degrees to 85 out of a possible 100. You are doing so well and, as a direct result of what you have just done, **you will have markedly more self-belief when running from now on**.

Now for the last of the three slider controls. This one is labelled, 'Number of Thought Threads' and this describes the number of streams of thought that run through your mind whilst running all of which drain your reserves of energy. As you can see this slider control is set quite high at 73 out of a possible 100. I'd like you to bring that down by moving the slider control to the left down to 5 out of a possible 100. You know what to do, **you know how to do this**. Focus and concentrate on the slider control for Number of Thought Threads, please, and move that all the way down to just 5 out of a possible 100. That's it. Keep it moving, nearly there, brilliant. Well done. Now, **whenever you run, your mind will be unified, quiet, crystal clear and sharply focussed**.

And now, let's look at the readout at the top of the screen and you can see that **your success in quietening down your inner chatter whilst running has increased**

your accessible stamina, by another 10 out of a possible 100 all the way up to 95 out of a possible 100, from where it was originally at 66 out of a possible 100. **You have now successfully increased your stamina levels by almost half as much again whilst running,** a huge improvement and a wonderful achievement.

So, now that you've changed the amount of stamina to which you have access whilst running it's time to make sure that they don't get changed back again accidentally and also ensure that your system settings are fully backed-up on the cloud.

This is a very straightforward thing to do. Look to the bottom of the screen you and you can clearly see a button labelled as 'Advanced Settings'. And, as you concentrate on that button the contents of the screen now change in front of your eyes and the 'Advanced Settings' controls are now in *your* control. Now concentrate on the checkbox marked 'Make changes permanent' and you can now see that turn from off to on. Wonderful. That means, **you will always now have markedly increased stamina when running.** Excellent.

And now for the last and final part of this process, the last and final part of what you need to do today to ensure that, **your increase in stamina is now permanent.**

Now your settings have been changed you can, **make certain that they don't get changed back again,** accidentally and also ensure that your system settings are fully backed-up on the cloud. Again this is a very straightforward thing to do. Look to the bottom of the screen you and you can clearly see a button labelled as

'Advanced Settings'. And, as you concentrate on that button the contents of the screen now change in front of your eyes and the 'Advanced Settings' controls are now in *your* control. Now concentrate on the checkbox marked **'Increase my stamina levels permanently and backup these settings to the cloud'** Focus and concentrate on this button for me pleas and turn it to ON, that's it, good, well done, and you can see that turn from off to on and watch the progress bar as everything is uploaded and backed up to the cloud. First class! Everything is now backed up to the cloud. You have done so well.

And now the process is complete. You have updated your Stamina app and changed your internal settings and, because you have done this, **you now have so much more stamina from which to draw when running**.

As you are changing into your running shoes before a run you will subconsciously go up the seven steps of STAMINA: **Strength, Tenacity, Attitude, Mindfulness, Inspiration, Nerve, Achievement, weaving all of these concepts into your sense of self.**

As you mentally climb the seven steps of STAMINA you, **call all of the strands of your personality together**. The various facets of your personality all look in one direction, all hands are to the pumps, **all extra-curricular streams of thought are brought to a close for each running session**, your focus becomes one of pinpoint clarity and, **your self-belief is solid and resilient**. Whilst the body functions at its full potential, **your mind will be crystal clear and deeply calm bringing about a state of elevated bliss as you run.**

Once the event has begun, words are no longer needed here. All internal chatter has come to an end. All trains of thought merge, become silent and begin to run along the same track on which you run yourself. You are unified in both personality and in purpose and this is evident in your level of focussed concentration on your task - **single-pointed, sharp, calm, clear, quiet and utterly determined.**

The mechanics of running do not need to be monitored or controlled by the conscious mind. And so, all of this, from the point of view of the conscious mind, will be automatic and flow naturally. Every time you run your breathing is finely tuned to precisely what your body and mind need and this is automatic, fully monitored and properly applied by your unselfconscious mind, your deeper mind. And, because of this, as you run, all stress and tension built up since your last run will simply melt away, **your mind solving problems unconsciously each and every time you run now.**

You've also ensured that, **these changes will remain permanent** and you've backed up the entire operating system to the cloud so that you can't lose your new settings no matter what happens. And, **Because of this, you will now always have markedly increased stamina when running.**

And now, having done all of this good work I would like to speak directly to your subconscious.

I would like to thank you for all the good work you do for CLIENT and I would like to thank you for listening to me. You now have the opportunity to vastly improve

CLIENT's overall experience by ensuring the full success of today's session.

When CLIENT is about to embark on a running session CLIENT changes his/her shoes into footwear more appropriate for the task in hand. During this process of changing shoes the increasing of STAMINA levels will also take place according to the changes CLIENT made today on his/her STAMINA app. Once CLIENT has completed his/her change of shoes he/she will be ready to run with the increased stamina levels as updated today. CLIENT's mind will become crystal clear and all irrelevant trains of thought will disappear from consciousness for the period of the running session. All strands of CLIENT's personality will be woven into a single unified strand with a single point of focus, temporarily shutting down all wasted streams of energy. Because of this CLIENT will have extra energy from which to draw and will also be immune to any negativity or doubtful voices whose views are not based on direct evidence from the body.

I ask all of you now to kindly ensure as well and as fully as I know that you can, and I know this, because, *you have all power here*, that, all of these suggestions are now embedded deeply into CLIENT'S mind at all levels, including waking consciousness, dreaming and day-dreaming and this will ensure that CLIENT will thrive and survive as is your true desire for CLIENT to do.

I am so very grateful to you for listening to me, for your attention and for your wonderful and necessary co-operation throughout all of this. Without you none of this could be possible. Because of you and your invaluable supportive role, CLIENT has been successfully able to change and that change is now complete and permanent.

Thank you!

In a minute I'm going to count from one to ten and, as you hear me say each number, you will become progressively more comfortable and happy with your new outlook, your new feelings. You, feel and notice, a growing certainty that, increased stamina is now a core part of your being and your personality.

And, when I reach the number ten, but not yet, you will open your eyes and feel and remember clearly that life truly is full of promise again, feeling deeply that fundamental and lasting changes have taken place for the better meaning that just being you is simply the most wonderful experience. Quiet optimism and calm but deep positivity are now integral to the foundations of your psyche. But before I start the count I'd like to inform you of something that I didn't tell you before. Because of the changes you have made today you now also, have increased depths of patience with others, and, simply because of this, your stress levels will naturally drop and your stamina will be sustained further.

Each morning you will awake feeling refreshed, optimistic and so very, very positive about your life. Wonderful. Well done.

And, if you ever choose to come to me for hypnosis again, you will slip into deep hypnosis gladly and easily, responding especially well to all of the suggestions that I make to you.

And so I begin the count:

    1 coming up
    2 feeling returning
    3 consciousness rising
    4 optimism beginning to flower
    5 beginning to feel awake
    6 joyful energy flooding through you
    7 overall positivity flowing now
    8 beginning to open your eyes
    9 opening your eyes
    10 fully awake and ready for anything

Go to sleep exduction:

And now, having carried out all of the necessary change, you can trust your unselfconscious to accept and permanently put into place all of the suggestions introduced today.

In a moment I am going to count to three and, when you hear the number three, you will fall into a deep and peaceful sleep and enter the natural sleep cycle and, when you awake, at the time of your choosing, you will feel fresh, confident, optimistic and very happy to be alive and very happy to be you.

And so, because of all that you have successfully achieved today, **life truly is full of promise for you again**, and you clearly see and appreciate that, **throughout your being on every level fundamental and lasting changes have taken place for the better,** meaning that, **just being you is simply the most wonderful experience.** Quiet optimism, increased stamina and deep, calm positivity are now integral to the foundations of your psyche.

But before I start the count I'd like to inform you of something that I didn't tell you before. Because of the changes you have made today you now also, **have increased depths of patience with others,** and, simply because of this, **your stamina levels will naturally rise and your clarity of mind will be sustained even further.**

And so I begin the count.

1... 2... 3... Sleep deeply now...

Increasing Self Confidence

You step over the threshold and into the most delightful room you have ever seen. You sense an atmosphere of deep and quiet calm. There, in the centre of the room you see an old fashioned wooden desk and next to it a leather arm chair. You walk over and sit down. And there, sitting on the desk in front of you, you see an electronic device similar in appearance to a large smartphone.

Pick it up, please and hold it. It has a reassuring weight and feels strangely comfortable in your hands, **doesn't it?** The screen lights up as the device becomes active. It has done this automatically because it recognises you. It is responding to you because, **this is your device**. What you presently hold in your hand is your inner controls device.

And, as you look at the screen you see that it's large and bright and, much like a phone or a tablet screen, this screen has many icons on it. It's a big screen, a bright screen and it is your screen and all of the apps on this screen are your personal internal apps running on your own personal operating system. These apps control your inner workings, how you live and how you experience you your life. And they contain the settings for what makes up your personality - how you feel, what you think, your personal preferences, your habits, your inclinations, what you like, what you don't like, and all of those kinds of personal things you'd expect to find on such a device.

And, just like all apps, the apps on this device can be configured in different ways according to the wishes of the owner. And, since the apps you see in front of you now are your apps, you can easily change your experience in this world and, **become naturally confident and unself-conscious,** simply by updating your internal app settings. And that's such good news, isn't it?

And, since you are doing this today, here in this place, *because* you have been suffering *needlessly* from a lack of self-confidence, at this point, I'd like to ask your endlessly resourceful unselfconscious mind to, **kindly revisit each and every, thought, symbol, feeling and memory related to your experience of low self-confidence,** that's right.

And, whilst you, **attend to this vital matter at an** unselfconscious **level,** you can now, **return your conscious attention to the device in your hand,** and have a look at one of those apps in particular and, **regain full and natural confidence in your abilities and yourself.**

And, whilst I guide you in doing that, I'd like your unselfconscious mind to look within and, **kindly search for, make ready and apply all of the understanding, abilities, strategies and attitudes necessary and appropriate to re-establish you in full confidence in all that you do, feel and think.**

Excellent, now, if you would look again at the screen on your device, please.

Right there in the centre of the screen in front of you, just where you'd expect it to be, you can see a bright icon with a little picture of your face in the middle of it. This is your 'Self-Confidence app' and this app contains the settings for all of those things that you think and feel about yourself and particularly how you feel about being in certain social situations. And you can clearly see that the little picture of yourself is not a smiley emoticon - it's a combination of a sad and nervous emoticon. But this isn't a problem because, **it's easy for you to become self-confident.** And you can, **start to do that right now**.

Let's open this up immediately, **because,** you'll soon see that, **it's easy for you to increase your self-confidence,** and, **start to feel really good about yourself**. Yes, and soon you find that you will, **feel naturally calm, feel quietly confident**, and, **be completely in control of your responses right away**.

And, since this is your screen with your apps and, **you are in full control of this process,** all you need to do is concentrate on the app and just will it to open for you. And so, if you could do that for me now, please, just focus your mind on the 'Self-Confidence' app, the bright icon with the little picture of your face in the middle of it and just will it to open. Good, that's right, and you can see that your 'Self-Confidence app' is opening now.

Now the app is fully open and it fills the whole of the screen and it shows a range of different controls for all of those things which you can change about yourself so that you can, **become a confident person simply by**

153

changing your internal settings on your Self Confidence app.

As you can see, the screen is split in half into two main sections - one at the top and one at the bottom. The section at the top shows three different slider controls. Each of the three slider controls take up the width of the screen with the lowest setting, zero or minimum to the left and the highest setting, one hundred or maximum, to the right. They work in exactly the same way as the volume slider control or the brightness slider control you are used to using on your smart phone. So, you'll find this very easy and straightforward.

The first of these is your 'Self-Acceptance' slider control and you can see clearly now that it's at a very low setting down at around just 15 out of a possible 100. And now, if you look at the slider below that you can see that this one is labelled as 'Self-Forgiveness' and that too is set very low at around 20 out of a possible 100. And the third and last one in this section is labelled 'Self-Seriousness' and you can see that this one is different to the previous two in that it is set too high at nearly 90 out of a possible 100.

So, as you can see, all of this is very clear. At the moment, due to your current settings, it seems that your previous lack of confidence had to do with you having too little love for yourself, finding it hard to forgive yourself and taking yourself very seriously. And while this is not at all unusual, it's certainly not necessary and, **you will have access to increased confidence once you have updated your settings**, on your app. And, what's more, **it's very easy for you to**

change these settings. You see, when you change the settings on your Self-Confidence app it automatically changes the way you feel about yourself. **It's easy for you to make this kind of change,** so, I'd like you to get ready to, **do just that right now, please.**

I'd like you to look at the screen again and see the three slider controls in the top half of the window. As previously mentioned you can see that they are labelled 'Self-Acceptance', 'Self-Forgiveness' and 'Self-Seriousness'.

Look at the first of the slider controls on in this list for me now, please, the one you can see is labelled 'Self-Acceptance' which you notice is set at only 15 out of a possible 100. Now, since this is your app on your personal device all you need to do is to will the slider to move to the right and you will see it start to move and the value begin to increase. Concentrate and focus on making it do that now, please. That's right. Good. You can see it has started moving to the right now. Keep it moving until it gets up to at least 90 out of a possible 100, that's it. Keep it going, nearly there… Wonderful. You've done it. And now you, **feel a glowing warmth inside**. A division inside you is disappearing. You are beginning to, **feel whole again, accept yourself, trust yourself and have natural confidence in your own being naturally.** And that's a lovely feeling, isn't it? So good, and so easy to achieve. You're doing *so* well! **You have every reason to feel confident,** now that you, **accept who you are so much more.**

And now that, **you've increased your sense of 'Self-Acceptance',** you can now move down to the next slider control, the one that you see underneath, the one that's labelled 'Self Forgiveness' which is set at only 20 out of a possible 100. **Increase this setting**, and you will, **regain natural faith in your own self**, because, increasing this setting will allow you to, **fully believe in your own worth,** again. Concentrate on that slider control now, please, and, in exactly the same manner that you did before with the 'Self-Acceptance' slider control, I'd like you to will the 'Self Forgiveness' slider control to move to the right from where it is right now at 20 out of a hundred all the way up to over 90 out of a hundred. Just focus and concentrate on it and will it to move to the right and it will. Good, that's it starting to move now. Keep going, keep it moving, all the way up. Nearly there - excellent! You've done it. And you can now see that your sense of 'Self Forgiveness' is now right up there at just over 90 out of a possible 100. You're really getting the hang of this. And, now, because of what you have just done you can, **feel inner comfort and self-acceptance expanding now. A long-held tension is fast disappearing. Trust in yourself has returned**. And that's a truly wonderful thing. And again, **so easy for you to do**. So, let's keep up your good work and move onto the last of the three slider controls in the upper half of the screen.

The third slider control is labelled 'Self Seriousness'. Now, as you can see, this one is set too high. You can see that's it gone all the way up to more than 90 out of 100 which means you have become overly serious about exactly who you are. This leads to difficulty when you wish to change and so lowering this will not only allow you to, **become more flexible in your responses to difficult situations,** but also to, **become**

more light-hearted about life in general. As someone once said, the reason that angels can fly is because they take themselves so lightly.

Let's fix this now and you can do it in exactly the same way that you did with the other two slider controls except this time you're going to move the Self-Seriousness slider control all the way down to the mid-20s out of a possible 100. Do this and you'll find that, **your life is full of promise and possibilities**. OK, you know what you're doing, you know how to do this. Concentrate and focus on that slider control for me now, please, and begin to move it to the left. Lovely, so good, you're becoming expert at this now. You can see the slider moving towards the left hand side of the screen as that number lowers. And, as you move the slider to the left and the number gets steadily lower you can, **feel the corresponding change inside,** which means you, **feel increasingly more accepting of yourself and your life as a whole,** and, because of this, indeed as a direct result of what you're doing now you can, **feel much more appreciative of all the good things in your life,** and, you, **notice all of the positive things now**. So good! **A warm, happy and contented feeling is growing naturally within you,** now, as you can feel. **Feel that deeply and know that this is how you're going to feel as a matter of course from now on**.

You have done so well and you've made some truly fundamental changes to how you feel about your life as a whole, allowing you to, **feel increasingly more positive and content about life and about yourself.**

And, now that you've made these important changes you're just about to, **make these changes permanent,** so that your new settings will remain set for good.

I'd like you to look now to the bottom half of the screen below the three slider controls that, **you've just successfully changed,** to make your life so much better.

Below those you can see one last slider control and three 'OFF/ON' buttons

Look at this last slider control. The slider control you are looking at right now is your 'Self-Consciousness' slider control. This is a crucial control. You can clearly see that this is set very high indeed and you will become so much happier within yourself in all situations when you, **lower the value of your 'Self-Consciousness' setting.** And so, I would like you to do that right now in order that, **your feelings of self-consciousness in any social situation is hardly noticeable.**

Concentrate and focus 'Self-Consciousness' slider control for me now, please, and begin to move it towards the left. Focus and concentrate, please, and just will it to move to the left. That's it, good. You can see the slider moving towards the left hand side of the screen now. And, as you move the slider control for 'Self-Consciousness' all the way to the left and the setting gets steadily lower you can, **feel the corresponding change inside,** which means you, **feel your self-consciousness disappearing and your inner comfort level rising,** and, as a direct result of what you're doing now you can, **dispense with feelings of self-consciousness altogether.** You have just made a

wonderful and fundamental change to your daily experience. Fantastic. You're nearly there.

Below the 'Self-Consciousness' slider control that you've just successfully updated you can see the three ON/Off buttons I mentioned earlier. All three of these On/Off buttons are presently set to OFF. Once you turn them from OFF to ON your experience of life will improve noticeably. So please have a look at these three buttons now.

The top one is labelled 'Lock slider controls for this app' and I'd like you to focus on that button now, please, and switch it from OFF to ON. Just concentrate on it and it will change. That's right. Well done. This means that **you feel so much more positive about yourself, your abilities and your prospects from now on**. Wonderful. And just how it should be. But, most importantly, you've also reduced your 'Self-Consciousness' to the minimum and this setting has also now been locked. **Self-consciousness will no longer trouble you** in any way.

Ok, two buttons to go. The second button in the list of three is labelled 'Overall Positivity'. You can see that this one is also set to OFF. You know what to do. Focus on the button, please, and turn it from OFF to ON. Do that now for me please. Excellent. And **now you instantly feel so much more positive**. The third and last button is labelled 'Inner Light'. Focus and concentrate on that one for me now, please and turn that one from OFF to ON. Well done. Now that your 'Inner Light' is on, **you feel a growing sense of being clean and fresh and new inside**. The shadows and the gloom are receding and the bright light of simple delight is illuminating your mind through and through. Your future is something to look forward to now. **Feel how lovely that is. Feel that deeply. See that. Be that. Like a flower opening its petals again after a long shower.** So good.

See, I told you it was easy. You just needed to want to change enough, and, since you have come here today and you have carried out such good work, it's clear that you really do want to, **change for the better. And thus it is so**. Life is so much easier and so much more enjoyable for you now; big things, little things, everything.

Ok. Now that you have managed to do all of that so successfully I'd like you now to close the app and then open up your 'whole psyche' app, which is the app that you can see now that is a wee icon of you with a smiley face. That's the one. Concentrate and focus on that app now, for me please. That's it. That's right and now you can see that the app is now fully open.

You can clearly see three slider controls in this app. The one at the top is labelled 'Inner Peace', the middle one is labelled 'Ability to Relax Fully' and the last one is labelled 'Quiet Optimism'. All of these, as you can see are set at very low levels but, **you can change these now**.

You know what to do. Focus and concentrate on these slider controls and move them from the left where they are set at low levels, move them from those low levels to the right of the screen to much, much higher levels. Do that for me now, please. First the 'Inner Peace' slider control. Move that one all the way up to maximum for me, please. **You know how to do this.** That's right, all the way. Good. The next one is 'Ability to Relax Fully'. Do the same with this one, please, and move it all the way up to maximum too. **You know how to do this too.** Superb. This seems so easy for you now and soon you'll have a very new outlook and it was all so straightforward for you to do. And now for the last slider control in this list, the one labelled 'Quiet Optimism'. Just as before, off you go, all the way to maximum… and you've done it.

Now, **feel these changes deeply. Embed these new feelings and attitudes into your daily outlook.** You know, **you feel so very differently now; confident and calm, each and both of you,** and because, **you now feel so very differently about everything,** you now know with absolute certainty that, **you have found your centre of confidence from which all good feeling arises.** Feel the relief now and feel the old energy and enthusiasm returning to you and filling you up. So good!

And now, lastly, just to ensure that you have fundamentally changed your outlook for the better, making you feel so much more positive and happy about your life and that even changes to your own personal internal operating system will mean that you will, **remain effortlessly positive and content about your life and about who you are** you need to turn the last button, the one labelled 'Backup App Settings to the Cloud', from OFF to ON.

And if you would do that for me now, please. Focus and concentrate on that last button, the one that will ensure your success in all of these beneficial changes today. Focus and concentrate on that button, please.

161

Focus and concentrate on this button for me pleas and turn it to ON, that's it, good, well done, and you can see that turn from off to on and watch the progress bar as everything is uploaded and backed up to the cloud. First class! Everything is now backed up to the cloud. **You are now a quietly confident, calm and happy individual.** Excellent.

The changes have been made. You now have a completely new and positive outlook on life, one that's so much more optimistic and full of energy than before and you've also ensured that, **you have made thes changes permanent** by ensuring your settings backup system has been turned on so that, **these settings will now stay set.** You have done so incredibly well and I'm so very pleased for you.

You, **feel a new peace within**, you, **feel centred in quiet confidence**, in all that you say and do and this is truly wonderful and no more than you truly deserve - a deep and lasting peace that becomes more and more established as, **natural confidence grows within you as each day passes**, which means that, **your feelings of self-consciousness in any social situation have been vastly reduced.** Feel that deeply now. **Feel now this change that has a permanent effect.** Feel just how magical this is. **Know,** that, **this is permanent now,** and you can therefore, **be joyful in your new identity.** And this is just the beginning.

Natural and easy self-confidence is now growing steadily within you and all remaining inner tension has simply evaporated away, leaving you feeling free and optimistic and full to the brim of delightful energy and enthusiasm about life. **This is your new identity.** You feel so much better all over and through and through and **this is all simply a normal and consistent part of who you are now.**

And now, I'd like you to practise being this new self-confident self of yours in all of the situations in life you can imagine, whilst I speak directly to your deeper mind, your other mind, the version of you that is your wiser self.

I am now speaking directly to your wiser self. Firstly I'd like to thank you for listening to me but more importantly I'd like to thank you for all that you do and all that you have done to keep CLIENT safe and well for so long.

Kindly implementing and reinforcing all of the suggested changes you have heard today regarding confidence is an easy and straightforward way to ensure that you, continue to provide this care to CLIENT, which will allow CLIENT ongoing and growing success and stability in this world.

This is your part: Kindly now take all of what you have heard and learned today and make it an integral part of CLIENT'S identity, outlook and attitude to life. Since it is true that, confidence breeds success, and that it's also true that, success is CLIENT'S goal, and this simply means that increasing CLIENT'S confidence fulfils the needs of each and both of you.

Please permanently increase CLIENT'S interest in and desire for regular exercise and CLIENT'S interest in good, healthy, nutritious food.

I ask all of you now to please, ensure as well and as fully as I know that you can, and I know this, because, *you have all power here*, that, all of these suggestions are now embedded deeply into CLIENT'S mind at all levels, including waking consciousness, dreaming and day-dreaming and this will ensure that CLIENT will not only survive but also thrive, *as is your true desire for CLIENT to do.*

I am so very grateful to you for listening to me, for your attention and for your wonderful and necessary co-operation throughout all of this. Without you none of this could be possible. Because of you and your invaluable supportive role, CLIENT has been successfully able to change and that change is now complete and permanent.

Thank you!

In a minute I'm going to count from one to ten and, as you hear me say each number, you will become progressively more comfortable and happy with your new outlook, your new feelings. You, feel and notice, a growing certainty that, quiet confidence is now a core part of your personality.

And, when I reach the number ten, but not before, you will open your eyes and feel and remember clearly that life truly is full of promise again, feeling deeply that fundamental and lasting changes have taken place for the better meaning that just being you is simply the most wonderful experience. Quiet optimism and calm but deep positivity are now integral to the foundations of your psyche. But before I start the count I'd like to inform you of something that I didn't tell you before. Because of the changes you have made today you now also, have increased depths of patience with others, and, simply because of this, your stress levels will naturally drop and your confidence will be sustained further.

Each morning you will awake feeling refreshed, optimistic and so very, very positive about your life. Wonderful. Well done.

And, if you ever choose to come to me for hypnosis again, you will slip into deep hypnosis gladly and easily, responding especially well to all of the suggestions that I make to you.

And so I begin the count:

   1 coming up
   2 feeling returning
   3 consciousness rising
   4 optimism beginning to flower
   5 beginning to feel awake
   6 joyful energy flooding through you
   7 overall positivity flowing now
   8 beginning to open your eyes
   9 opening your eyes
   10 fully awake and ready for anything

Go to sleep exduction:

And now, having carried out all of the necessary change, you can trust your unselfconscious to accept and permanently put into place all of the suggestions introduced today.

In a moment I am going to count to three and, when you hear the number three, you will fall into a deep and peaceful sleep and enter the natural sleep cycle and, when you awake, at the time of your choosing, you will feel fresh, confident, optimistic and very happy to be alive and very happy to be you.

And so, because of all that you have successfully achieved today, **life truly is full of promise for you again**, and you clearly see and appreciate that, **throughout your being on every level fundamental and lasting changes have taken place for the better**, meaning that, **just being you is simply the most wonderful experience**. Quiet optimism and deep, calm positivity are now integral to the foundations of your psyche.

But before I start the count I'd like to inform you of something that I didn't tell you before. Because of the changes you have made today you now also, **have increased depths of patience with others,** and, simply because of this, **your stress levels will naturally drop and your confidence will be sustained even further.**

Now you, **have extra patience and understanding with the world and all of the people in it than you've ever had before.**

And so I begin the count.

1... 2... 3... Sleep deeply now...

Weight Loss

And now the scene changes and you walk into the most beautiful room you have ever seen. In the centre of the room, underneath an ornate chandelier, sits an old fashioned wooden desk and a leather arm chair. Please go across to the table and take a seat. On the desk you see an electronic device similar in appearance to a large smart-phone.

You pick it up and find that it feels just right in your hand. You also notice that it has a pleasant, reassuring weight to it. The screen lights up as the device becomes active. It has done this automatically because it recognises you. It is responding to you because, **this is your device**. What you presently hold in your hand is your inner controls device.

Your device has a large screen much like a smart phone but slightly bigger. And, much like those types of screen, this screen has many app icons on it. It's a big screen, it's a bright screen and it is your screen and all of the apps on this screen are your personal apps running on your own personal operating system. These apps relate to how you live and experience your life and they contain the settings for what makes up your personality - how you feel, what you think, your personal preferences, your contacts and all those kinds of personal things you'd expect to find on such a screen.

And, just like all apps, these apps can be configured in different ways according to the wishes of the owner. And, since the apps you see in front of you now are your apps, you can easily change your experience in this world and, **regain full control over your eating**, simply and easily, **by updating your internal app settings.**

And, since you are doing this today, here in this place, *because* you have been suffering *needlessly* from overeating, at this point, I'd like to ask your endlessly resourceful unselfconscious mind to, **kindly revisit each and every, thought, symbol, feeling and memory related to your unhappy relationship to food and eating,** that's right.

And, whilst your unselfconscious mind is carrying out this task, you can now return your attention to the device in your hand and have a look at one of those apps in particular and, **regain full control over what you eat and how much you eat.**

And, whilst I guide you in doing that, I'd like your unselfconscious mind to look within and, **kindly search for, make ready and apply all of the understanding, abilities, strategies and attitudes necessary and appropriate to comprehensively reform your relationship to food and eating into a happy one for the rest of your life.**

Excellent, now, if you would look again at the screen on your device, please.

In the very centre of the screen in front of you, you can see a round, yellow icon with a tiny image of a set of cutlery in the middle of it. This is your '**Eating**' app and this app contains all of the settings for your appetite concerning different food stuffs; how much you like to eat, the size of your stomach, things like that. Changing the settings on this app will allow you to easily, **reduce the amount you eat to sensible levels permanently.**

Let's open that app now and see what can be changed so that, **you can easily readjust your relationship with food**. And, since this is your screen with your apps and since, **you are in complete control of this process,** all you need to do is simply concentrate on the app and will it to open for you.

And so, if you could do that for me now, please, just focus mentally on the 'Eating' app, the round, yellow icon with a wee picture of a set of cutlery the middle of it. Good, that's right, and your 'Eating' app is opening now.

This is good news because having seen that the app has responded and opened just because of your focussing on it and this means that, **you can easily change and update your internal app settings,** and, **you will therefore find success very straightforward today because of that.**

You can see now that you 'Eating' app is open and it fills the whole of the screen and it is shows a range of different controls for all those things which affect your relationship to food and eating.

And, the first thing we can see on the screen now that your 'Eating' app is opened is a slider control just like the slider control you're already familiar with that you use for increasing or decreasing the brightness on your smart phone but this slider control you can see in front of you now right at the top of the screen allows you to increase or decrease the size of your stomach.

Now, you can see some words above the slider control with extra information. As you can see now, it says ,'The stomach size slider control is locked. To unlock this control first eliminate all psychological triggers that lead to over-eating, binge-eating and emotional eating. Press this red button to open'.

Ok, so now you know that in order to be able to reduce the size of your stomach you must first open your settings for 'Psychological Triggers for Eating' and remove all the Triggers there. Let's do that now. See the red button beneath the slider control for 'Stomach Size'. Concentrate and focus on that red button for me now, please, and the 'Psychological Triggers' controls will open for you. Just focus and concentrate on that button, please, and just will it to open. That's it. Well done. As you can see it's opening now and it fills up the whole screen.

Since we know that psychological triggers can make you want to eat more than you actually need to eat you're going to find that when you adjust these controls, **you will only want to eat when you are truly hungry**, which means that, **from now on you will only want to eat when your body needs food**.

So, let's look now at the screen and see what you can change to make yourself happy inside and out and eliminate any unnecessary urges to eat too much.

Now, as you can see the screen shows a list of sliders and the first one in the list is labelled as 'Worries About the Past' and this one is set quite high towards the right of the screen. And, since you know that you can't change what's happened in the past, you therefore know that, **there's no point at all in having any worries about your past,** so you can move this slider control all the way to the left until it's at Minimum. Do that for me now, if you would, please. Just focus and concentrate on the slider control for 'Worries About the Past' and just will it to move it all the way towards the left hand side of the screen. That's it, good, you can see it moving now and you will also feel a corresponding reduction in inner tension because of that. Keep it moving, all the way to the left. Excellent. You've done it. You're now so much less concerned about what happened in the past.

Good. Now we can move on to the next slider control underneath and this one is labelled 'Worries About the Future'. This one is set very high as well, but, since you know that, **there's no point at all in worrying about an unknown future,** I'd like you to do exactly the same with this slider control as you've just done with the slider control for 'Worries About the Past'. Just focus and concentrate on the slider control and just will it to move all the way to the left to the lowest setting possible. Do that for me now, please. Just focus and concentrate on the slider control and move this all the way to the left. That's right, you can see it moving to the left now towards minimum. Keep it going, that's right, excellent, you've done it. The slider control for 'Worries About the Future' is now set to Minimum and you, **feel so much better inside**, already. And that's a lovely feeling, isn't it?

Good. **Now you've successfully eliminated all worries about the past and the future** you can go onto the next slider control here. If you look you can see now that the next slider control in this list is labelled 'Overall

173

Contentedness with Life'. And, as you can see, this slider control is set too far to the left. Let's move it all the way to the right and, **become more content with your life overall.** Just concentrate and focus on that slider control in the same way that you did with the other two but this time you're going to move it all the way to the right. So, just focus and concentrate on the slider control for 'Overall Contentedness with Life' and just will it to move towards the right. That's right, excellent. You can see it now and you'll also be able to feel a warm feeling of contentedness inside as the slider moves all the way to maximum. Keep going, that's right. Excellent, you've done it. Your overall contentedness with life has been increased to the maximum and because of this you, **feel so much better about life already,** and, due to this, **your appetite has already decreased**. You're doing so well.

ecause you have reduced your worry to the minimum and increased your 'Overall Contentedness with Life' to the maximum you can, **feel a growing sense of happiness begin to appear in your stomach**. Feel that wonderful feeling now, see its warm colour now, and notice that it's expanding and filling you up. You feel a lovely feeling of peace within you now. Wonderful, wonderful, wonderful.

And that's the secret - when you're filled up with happiness inside, your desire to fill yourself up with food just disappears because there's just no room for it.

Good. Now, all you have to do next is to focus and concentrate on the 'Back' button in the top left-hand corner of the screen and you can return to the 'Stomach Size' control slider. Do that for me now please. Just focus and concentrate on the 'Back' button in the top left-hand corner of the screen, please. That's it, well done. And now you can see that the Stomach Size control slider is now unlocked because you have removed all of your 'Psychological Triggers for Eating'.

You are now ready to reduce the size of your stomach. You can clearly see that the slider control for 'Stomach Size' is set all the way to the right near Maximum. In a minute you're going to move that slider to the centre, to half way and, when you do that, **the size of your stomach is going to reduce by half**. Can you feel the excitement rising within you? You are just about to make the most wonderful change in your life.

Now, you know what to do. Just focus and concentrate on the slider control for 'Stomach Size' and will it to move left until it gets to the centre. Do that now, please. Focus, concentrate, that's it, you can see it starting to move to the left now. You're doing well, keep going, that's it moving now, keep going.... Excellent! You've done it. You've now reduced the size of your stomach by half. And you can now feel a corresponding strange but wonderful feeling inside.

And that feeling is the result of a combination of feeling so much more happy inside along with your stomach size being reduced by half. Feel those feelings deeply now. Feel that deep contentedness inside. Feel that, **your stomach is now so much smaller**. You, **feel so differently inside now**. So good!

Now, the next part is very important. Since you will only be eating half of what you used to eat because of the fact that, **your stomach is now so much smaller than it was before**, you will need to alter your internal settings about what type of food you eat to ensure that you get sufficient nutrition. **You know this is very important.** This is easy to do so I'd like you to, **do this now**.

Look back at the screen again and in the middle of it you can now see three more slider controls. The first slider control is labelled 'Good Nutritious Food' and this one is set in the middle between 'Minimum Attraction' on the left and 'Maximum Attraction' on the right. I want you now to increase your desire for 'Good Nutritious Food' by moving that slider control all the way to the right-hand side of the screen until it reaches 'Maximum Attraction'. Do that for me now, please. Focus and concentrate on the slider control and move it all the way to the right. Good, that's it, you can see it moving now, keep it going, all the way, excellent. You've done it. Now, because you've done this you will now, **be attracted to 'Good Nutritious Food' whenever you feel hungry**.

Now, let's move on to the next slider control. This one is labelled 'Junk Food' and your slider control for 'Junk Food' is set to 'Maximum Attraction'. You're going to move that slider control all the way to the left until it gets to 'Minimum Attraction'. You know what to do. Concentrate and focus on that slider control and move it to the left, all the way to 'Minimum Attraction'. Do that now, please. Concentrate and Focus. That's it. See it moving to the left. Keep going, you're doing so well, keep it moving to the left. Wonderful. You've done it. Now, whenever you get hungry you will be revolted the by even the thought of junk food. You only want to eat good food. 'Junk Food' revolts you now whilst 'Good

Nutritious Food' is so much more appealing. Now you find the idea of eating healthily very, very attractive because, now, **you've got the best of reasons for doing so.**

And now, the last slider control is labelled 'Interest in Regular, Healthy Exercise'. And, as you can see this one is set quite low near the left-hand side of the screen. I'd like you now to move the slider control for 'Interest in Regular Healthy Exercise' all the way to the right towards 'Maximum Attraction'. You know what to do. Focus and concentrate and move that slider control all the way to the right. See it moving, that's it. Wonderful. You've done it. You've set your desire for 'Interest in Regular Healthy Exercise' to 'Maximum Attraction' which means that, **your desire to exercise has increased hugely.** Now, **you want to exercise.** And you know you will get so much out of it when you do. How wonderful is that?

So, now, **because you have successfully updated your eating app settings which control your relationship to food,** and, **the size of your stomach has been reduced by half,** you should now make sure that, **this cannot be undone,** and also ensure that your system settings are fully backed-up to the cloud. Again, this is a very straightforward thing for you to do. Look to the bottom of the screen you and you can clearly see a button labelled as, '**Make these changes permanent**'. Turn this button on just by focussing and concentrating on it. Do that for me now, please. Focus, concentrate, that's it. Wonderful. You've now done exactly what's needed to, **make all these changes permanent.**

And now, so that you don't lose your new settings, I'd like you to turn the final button, the one labelled 'Back up Settings to the Cloud' from OFF to ON. Focus and concentrate on this button for me please and turn it to ON, that's it, good, well done, and you can see that turn from off to on and watch the progress bar as everything is uploaded and backed up to the cloud. First class! Everything is now backed up to the cloud.

So good!

And now the process is complete. **You have,** updated your Eating app settings and, **successfully changed your relationship to food and eating.** You've also ensured that, **these changes will remain permanent,** because you've backed up all of these changes to the cloud so that, **you cannot lose your new settings no matter what happens.** And you have done all of this yourself. You can now see and feel that, **you now have full control over how you feel about eating.**

As a direct result of how you have changed today, **you can now control your feelings of hunger,** and this clearly means that, **feelings of hunger will only arise when your body genuinely needs to ingest food.**

There is something more for you now: because you have done this all of this today, as a direct result of what you have done today **you are now so much happier inside than you were before. Your worries have been reduced to the minimum. You are now attracted to good nutritious food. The idea of eating junk food is now taboo.** And simply because of this, **Junk Food holds no interest for you at all.** And, because of this, **you are** therefore highly attracted by the idea of regular, healthy exercise. Additionally, **your stomach is now only half the size it was before you arrived today**.

I'd like now to speak to your other mind, your deeper mind. Firstly I'd like to thank you for all that you have done to keep CLIENT safe and well for so long.

I'd like you to understand and accept the importance of the twin laws of diminishing returns and of delayed gratification. CLIENT has forgotten that these two laws, which mean that the shorter the length of time we wait before repeat an action that we enjoy, the less enjoyable it becomes, or, to put it another way, the longer we can wait (and we can!) before doing something we enjoy, the more we will enjoy it when it's the proper time to do it.

Please, if you would, kindly bring these two concepts, these two laws, the law of diminishing returns and the law of delayed gratification out of the darkness and back into the light. See, understand and accept the deep wisdom of these two laws clearly now, please. [15 second pause] See their wonderful value to each and both of you. Kindly enthrone these ideas in both the forefront and the depths of CLIENT'S understanding. Incorporate these ideas, these values, these laws deeply in all areas of CLIENT'S psyche. They are great strengths of enormous worth. These are the reins that will pull CLIENT'S horses of desire away from the path of overindulgence. Their full acceptance and application are vital for a healthy and satisfactory life. Increase the importance of these laws so that they intimately inform CLIENT'S attitude towards the food that he/she puts into his/her body.

And, making this even easier for CLIENT, please understand that engaging in regular healthy exercise highly attractive, worthwhile and very, very enjoyable to contemplate and to engage in. Regular, healthy exercise is the magical cure for all sorts of negative feelings which can lead to over eating and over drinking. Regular, healthy exercise is truly such a wonderfully desirable and satisfying activity in which to engage.

In this way kindly decrease CLIENT'S appetites for food according to the changes to the app settings made today and in line with the two exceptionally important laws of diminishing returns and of delayed gratification whilst simultaneously increasing CLIENT'S interest in and desire for regular, healthy exercise. In doing this you will benefit [CLIENT] so much and a growing problem, will be easily solved.

I ask all of you now to kindly ensure as well and as fully as I know that you can, and I know this, because you have all power here, that, all of these suggestions are now embedded deeply into CLIENT'S mind at all levels, including waking consciousness, dreaming and day-dreaming and this will ensure that CLIENT will thrive and survive as is your true desire for CLIENT to do.

I am so very grateful to you for listening to me, for your attention and for your wonderful and necessary co-operation throughout all of this. Without you none of this could be possible. Because of you and your invaluable supportive role, CLIENT has been successfully able to change and that change is now complete and permanent.

Thank you!

Wake up exduction:

In a minute I am going to count to ten. As you hear each number you will feel more and more awake and more and more convinced of the success of this session.

When you hear the number 10, but not yet, you will be fully awake, your clarity of mind will be pristine and you will be filled to the brim with joyful energy, feeling as if you are capable of anything you set your mind to. You will feel this simply because, **this is true**.

Your relationship to food and eating has been transformed. You will only be able to eat half as much as you could before. You will find great, great delight in this. This feeling will increase as each day passes.

And, if you ever choose to come to me for hypnotherapy again, you will slip into deep hypnosis gladly and easily, responding especially well to all of the suggestions that I make to you.

And so, I begin the count…

1. Coming up
2. Feeling returning
3. Consciousness rising
4. Optimism beginning to flower
5. Beginning to feel awake
6. Joyful energy flooding through you
7. Overall positivity flowing now
8. Beginning to open your eyes

9. Opening your eyes
10. Fully awake and ready for anything

Go to sleep exduction:

And now, having carried out all of the necessary change, you can trust your unselfconscious to accept and permanently put into place all of the suggestions introduced today.

In a moment I am going to count to three and, when you hear the number three, you will fall into a gentle and peaceful sleep and enter the natural sleep cycle and, when you awake, at the time of your choosing, you will feel fresh, confident, optimistic and very happy to be alive and very happy to be you.

Your relationship to food and eating has been transformed. You will only be able to eat half as much as you could before. You will find great, great delight in this. This feeling will increase as each day passes.

And, if you ever choose to come to me for hypnotherapy again, you will slip into deep hypnosis gladly and easily, responding especially well to all of the suggestions that I make to you.

And so I begin the count…

1… 2… 3…